Don't stand under a tree when it rains.

An American's perspective on

life and business during the Egyptian uprising.

Marshall L. Stocker

ISBN: 0615832504
ISBN-13: 978-0615832500

For information and other requests please contact:
Marshall L. Stocker
marshall@marshallstocker.com

Disclaimer: This book is a work of non-fiction. I have tried to recreate events, locales, and conversations from my memories of them. However, the author and publisher specifically disclaim any liability, loss, or risk, whether personal, financial, or otherwise, that is incurred as a consequence, directly or indirectly, from the use and/or application of any contents of this book. In order to maintain the anonymity of characters, I have changed some names and identifying characteristics, such as physical descriptions and occupations. Finally, this is one version of events that transpired in the Middle East. It is not an authoritative analysis, simply one American's story about life and business during the Egyptian uprising.

CONTENTS

ACKNOWLEDGMENTS

This story would not exist without people.

I am grateful to my business partner, Howard Rich, and investors, who trusted me to lead our investment in Egypt. I am indebted to Mohamed El Sewedy, Nora Soliman, and Suzy Kamel for their wisdom on managing life and business in Cairo. Anita Anderson and Andrea Rich were helpful with their perspectives from afar. I have Governor David Beasley to thank for introducing me to the Middle East.

My Egyptian employees, Suzy Kamel, Tamer Hamdy, Shady Elewa, and Tarek Zakry, were capable, loyal, enthusiastic, and fun. They were the best a manager could have. I am thankful to my accountant, Samer Talaat Hanna, and his staff, along with my lawyers, Sara Hinton, Mohamed Nour, Heba El Naggar, and their paralegals, for explaining Egypt's bureaucracy and exposing me to it. I am fortunate that Christine Anwar and her colleagues were capable and exceedingly patient pedagogues, or I would have never learned to speak Arabic.

John Harris, Wendy Steavenson, Aaron DeLong, Angus Blair, Simon Kitchen, Ellen Brooks, TJ Quinn, Julie and Karl Hilberg, Steve Haley, João Terlica, my polo teammates, and all my expatriate friends deserve recognition. They helped me appreciate what happened to us and around us. Thank you.

I am obliged to Doug MacLean and Wendy Steavenson, whose persistent encouragement motivated me to turn a collection of experiences into this book. Talia Leduc deserves recognition for her skillful work and guidance as a copy editor.

For all the above, I have also my wife to thank. Alexandra trusted my decision to start a speculative venture in a country where I could not speak the language, save for the days I was caught in a revolution. She heard of my tribulations daily, and her sound advice and insightful opinions helped me overcome them. Thank you for everything, Ali.

1 IN THE SQUARE

Throughout the past few months in Egypt, I had often been an accidental witness to the uprising, but this time was different. This time, I went to Tahrir Square knowing there would be danger. Four days earlier, more than forty protestors had been killed by Egyptian police on Mohamed Mahmoud Street, and three hundred others had been arrested. The street accessed Tahrir Square, opposite the side from which we were approaching, and led to Egypt's loathed Ministry of the Interior, making it the front for clashes between dissidents and security forces. I worried that tonight might be no different than the previous evenings, when protestors had fought unsuccessfully to gain access to the Central Security Forces' headquarters. I had not yet made it across Qasr El Nil Bridge and could already smell the acrid scent of tear gas.

Just outside Tahrir Square, my friend Nora stopped to greet a fellow member of the social-liberal Justice Party. His face was chalk white, covered in a tear-gas antidote: baking soda. His safety goggles had left rings of exposed skin around his eyes, and perspiration had run in streaks down his forehead and cheeks. Recognizing Nora, he hunched over immediately and placed his hands on his knees, supporting his upper body as he breathed heavily and began confirming what I suspected: Protestors were again attacking the Ministry of the Interior, and police were fighting back, hurling tear gas and shooting dissidents with purportedly non-lethal projectiles.

Nora Soliman was an Egyptian-American. She had grown up in Egypt, where her Egyptian father was a leading medical doctor, and had travelled to the US for college. She had eventually returned to Egypt to work as a director for a foreign aid agency focused on education programs. Her fluency in colloquial Arabic evidenced her Egyptian nationality despite her exceptional height and straight blond hair. She had already participated in the historic January 2011 protests, which had led to the resignation of President Hosni Mubarak, and she knew many of the dissidents and the city well. With her quick pace along the twenty-minute route from her apartment, she had none of the apprehension that I did about going to Tahrir Square, where the evening's protests may have already turned violent. Perhaps her husband, John, shared my worry, as we were both lagging a meter behind her.

John Harris had become my closest friend in Cairo. A few weeks before the dissidents toppled them, John and I had together defeated Egypt's police force in a different venue, the polo field. He had a diplomatic personality, and I never knew him to interfere with the political ambitions of his wife, no matter how dangerous the protests she attended might become. The adventurous side of John's personality was much more subtle. He wrote restaurant reviews for a Cairo-based English newspaper and often eschewed fancy locales for more casual dining in the poorer neighborhoods of sub-Saharan immigrants. John was unmistakably American in appearance. His brown hair and blue eyes gave away the fact, as did his habit of wearing shorts and flip-flops against a backdrop of conservatively dressed Egyptians. John's height was his most camouflaging feature on that walk to Tahrir, as he stood a couple of inches shorter than I did.

For a mother of three, Nora was a bit cavalier, but I trusted her instinct. Ten months earlier, I had taken her advice to leave Egypt briefly amidst the most violent protests, which had broken the thirty-year stranglehold that Hosni Mubarak held on Egypt's presidency. Still, the mass of chalk-white faces I could see as I approached Tahrir scared me. During most large protests in Tahrir, citizens assembled at the various entrances to screen people trying to enter the square. The effort required a large amount of manpower, as there were at least eight routes into Tahrir. The amateur gatekeepers had strung up rope barriers in their attempt to keep troublemakers and weapons out of the square, but they were also quite suspicious of foreigners. That night, John surreptitiously made his way through security by confidently ducking under a rope, exemplifying his preference for asking for forgiveness rather than permission in Egypt. When I was stopped as I cautiously tried to make my way through, Nora successfully intervened with a cover story that I was a journalist, she my interpreter. The next morning, I made good on that white lie, as I penned a description of what I had witnessed in Tahrir.

As the tear-gas hangover from the night before began to wear off, I sent my record of the experience to my wife and my colleague, both of whom had repeatedly cautioned me against going anywhere near the protests, which were now happening several times a week. I spared them the most visceral details for more than a year, as my tolerant wife's indulgence of my adventures did have a limit. An excerpt from my email follows:

> I confess, I was in Tahrir last night. Had to finally get into the mix to really see what was going on. Went under the guidance of Nora. Not expecting to go back. Been there, done that. Have the graphic memories to last a lifetime.
>
> Point is, what's happening is real serious. All potential outcomes are on the table. Difficult to assign any probabilities. The numbers are HUGE in Tahrir.
>
> Reports tonight that "invisible" tear gas is being used, making for claims of crimes against humanity. I believe it

after having had a horribly runny nose just being in proximity to some tear gas that's already been reported to be much more potent than January's.

The people in Tahrir, I know, were not Muslim Brotherhood, though I did see some individual big-beards. MB today abstained from further dissidence and withdrew from protests, presumably to defend their interest in seeing elections ASAP.

This still might all lead to an ideological government, but those who have brought this about aren't ideological. They're trying to affirm John Locke's natural rights. I can't believe the current dissidents will ever enunciate such classic liberal theories, but I think they'll shun dictates from something like an MB coalition. They just seem to feel it.

Not sure I've distilled this well, but being on the square sure felt good. It felt like championing humanity, and I'm sure I felt only one quarter of what Egyptians felt. Somehow I think this leads to a centrist government, though there could be a longer period of instability than we expected.

That night, the scene in Tahrir was a carnival. There were street vendors selling everything from clothing with revolutionary slogans to refreshments, cigarettes, and cotton candy. Some had colorfully painted pushcarts, and the ingenious had illuminated their wares with pink and blue lighting powered by electricity drawn from nearby street lamps. The crowd was dense but navigable. The center of the square was a raised section of soil where those conducting a sit-in had staked claims for their tents and makeshift shelters. A handful of motorcycles were idling as their young pilots stood astride, seemingly waiting for assignments. I had seen images and videos of motorcycles ferrying injured protestors away from the front lines of the clashes, and I wondered what violence those young men would see that night.

We were on the lookout for our friend Wendy Steavenson and her translator. Wendy had arrived in Egypt about the time of Hosni Mubarak's resignation to pen feature stories for The New Yorker magazine. Her coverage of the events and people of the Egyptian uprising later earned her the prestigious title of staff writer for the publication. The product of an elite English education, Wendy had steered far from the path of her peers. She had moved to the country of Georgia, where she authored a book on the formerly communist nation's political transition at a time when economic insecurities had left electricity unavailable for but a few hours each day—she had learned that turning on her oven was the best way to heat her apartment. Her pocket-sized notebook was an inseparable possession that would appear almost without exception during coffees and dinners, and it was filled with haphazard scribbles that ran at odd angles on its faintly lined pages. That evening, Nora and I quickly spotted her in Tahrir wearing her usual attire of baggy chinos, Adidas sneakers, and an awkwardly large yellow sports watch in a country where no one was ever on time. None stood out from afar as I had expected. Rather, our beacon was her straight blond hair, which bobbed like a buoy in a sea of black.

Her Egyptian translator, Hassan El Naggar, would have been harder to spot but for his shoulder-length curly hair, which also sprouted upwards to make him several inches taller. In spite of his youth, his professional abilities meant Wendy guarded him jealously from other journalists. I had already met Hassan, having had several lengthy conversations during dinner parties Wendy had hosted. Surprisingly, he had never volunteered a memorable opinion of the uprising's events or characters. I sensed his passion lay elsewhere, and this was later confirmed when I learned of his appearance on the cover of an Egyptian newspaper. In the lead article, he was reported to be under police interrogation for being a Satanist. According to Egypt's post-uprising Muslim Brotherhood government, Hassan's role as guest singer in a hard rock band had purportedly proven that fact.

We loitered in Tahrir Square, unable to avoid inhaling the tear gas. If there was a "fog of war," the tear gas that had blown in from Mohamed Mahmoud Street and now hung over the square was Egypt's fog of revolution. Interrupting our voyeurism, a teenage boy stepped in front of John and me. He held out a tear gas canister, no larger than a soda can, labeled in English with "Made in the USA." It had been shot with such great force that it had been dented and its surface repeatedly scratched as it slid across the street. If the canister had hit someone during its arced descent, its force would have been sufficient to render a fatal injury, as had been reported in several prior instances.

Made in the U.S.A.: Spent tear gas canister accompanied by various ammunitions that Egyptian security forces purportedly used on dissidents (Photo by Floris Van Cauwelaert)

As if we were easy marks, another boy quickly stepped in front of me and raised a spray bottle toward my head. He mumbled something and, without waiting for a reply, sprayed me in the face with a cloudy white liquid. I immediately wiped it off with one hand while I reached with the other for my handkerchief, but Nora turned to explain that the boy had merely been trying to help protect me from the skin irritation caused by the tear gas. I left the remaining traces of baking soda, but I felt unnerved by the incident.

I heard a series of cheers from near the center of the square. Someone had been shouting phrases that a much larger group was repeating, and a group of teenage boys who had been responsible for the cheers assembled into two lines, clapping their hands in unison and running in place with their knees high. Each of the boys wore a mask over his mouth and nose, and some put on the goggles that had been dangling around their necks. Then they made their way, still in line, toward Mohamed Mahmoud Street, disappearing out of sight. They were going to the front line of the clashes where, days earlier, forty or so dissidents had been killed. I wondered whether some might not live through the night.

That night in Tahrir Square came little more than halfway through my time in Egypt. The ghostly scene of baking soda–covered faces had made the revolution seem suddenly all too real, and I realized that Egypt would be in for a long period of instability. That prediction proved correct: When I finally left Egypt more than a year later, the political situation was still irrefutably unstable. Until that night in Tahrir, though Nora had declared me a journalist to the vigilante guards, I had really been an American businessman with a real estate venture to run. Now, having literally seen blood in the streets, I was forced to consider whether I should keep investing in Egypt. Meanwhile, the ordinary business of life continued to so frequently turn my expectations upside down that the Arab Spring proved to be just one of many surprises I would encounter.

2 A SUITCASE FULL OF CASH

In late 2007, four years before I found myself standing in Tahrir Square with my face covered in baking soda, I invited a business acquaintance, Howard Rich, to join me for coffee in the grill room at the Yale Club of New York. Howie was a client of mine who had charged me with investing his stock portfolio, and I had profitably managed his investments until he fortuitously liquidated his account early in 2007, shortly before the global financial crisis.

We sat next to a lustrous copper-mantled fireplace, which reflected the room's vaulted ceiling. The walls were paneled in dark-stained wood, dotted with portraits of prestigious graduates that trumpeted their accomplishments. Glancing at them idly while we made ourselves comfortable, I felt as though I was being warned of the anonymity of mediocrity.

I had heard from others of Howie's reputation as a generous and dogged benefactor of free-market causes. I was also cautioned that he did not suffer fools—though nor did I. I got straight to the point: I needed a more fulfilling and exciting career, and perhaps Howie would have an idea as to what that might be.

We each came from completely different backgrounds. Howie had lived his whole life in Brooklyn and Manhattan, I in Indiana and far upstate in New York. He had never formally worked in the investment industry, as I had always done. His education came from starting and growing the litany of businesses he owned, whereas mine came from classes at Cornell University. I wore Gucci loafers without socks. He donned black lace-ups with rubber soles. His wife later confided in me that Howie almost always wore the same shoes and that he had purchased three additional pairs and stored them in his closet, reasoning that when his favorite shoes wore out, he did not want to find them discontinued, no longer for sale. Though he was approaching seventy years of age, Howie's mind was exceptionally sharp. He often jumped straight to what he saw as the crux of the matter, and he frequently used the forgetfulness associated with others his age to justify interrupting a conversation to ask a question.

The only thing I remember of our conversation was one such interruption. For my entire adult life, I had known how to respond to this question, but that day, I was at a loss when he asked, "What is it that you want to do?"

I was a bit peeved at this. I had planned to lay out my interests and have him give me the answer. If I knew the job title to which I was aspiring, I would be doing it, not asking for guidance. I decided to take a risk, as the answer I gave him could easily have made me a fool that Howie would not suffer.

"I wish I had been the guy who stepped off the airplane in Eastern Europe with a suitcase full of cash, you know, to buy poorly performing assets the day after the Wall fell, when the place became a free-market economy. That's what I want to do."

Howie reached for his cup and sipped his tea slowly. He was the kind of guy who always carried a few sachets of his favorite green tea in his pocket, never risking that a restaurant's offerings would prove inferior. After finishing the cup, he only promised to give some thought to my idea, and I left the club without any new career insights that day. Worse, I had no idea where to start satisfying my ambition now that I had said it out loud. After a couple of months passed following our meeting, I could only conclude that I had been the fool not suffered. Then Howie called me. He had recalled my previous experience working in the Middle East, and he thought I was the right guy to evaluate a potential investment project in Egypt.

Four years earlier, I had visited Yemen to deliver a series of lectures on how to attract investment by creating a more hospitable policy environment. It was the first country I would visit in the Middle East, and before I had even deplaned in Sana'a, the capital city, I had made the first of my misinformed expectations about life in the region.

As the plane touched the runway and slowed, passengers had clapped. We had arrived safely, with "Thanks be to God" muttered in Arabic by the locals around me, and I remember feeling bemused. Was safely landing a commercial aircraft a feat worthy of applause? Perhaps it was. The plane was remarkable mostly because it belonged to the national airline of one of the world's poorest countries. It was by far the oldest on which I had flown, only to be bested by an aged Russian plane on which I later flew in North Korea. Clearly, the mechanicals were in order, as we had arrived safely. However, the interior of the plane had suffered a worse fate. My seat felt as though it had been used for several decades, and little cushioning was left. Similarly, the bathroom door was nonfunctional, stuck halfway open—though those who heeded the call of nature hadn't seemed to mind.

Most people had stood up to unload their luggage from the overhead bins while the plane was still taxiing to the terminal. Western airlines had convinced me that it was dangerous to unbuckle my seatbelt before the plane came to a complete stop, and their flight attendants seemed compelled to remind travelers of this rule. The rules I had known in the West seemed to have no hold over the Middle East, and my common expectations, like a safe landing, warranted exceptional recognition. Such was my introduction to life and business in the region.

When we departed the airport, I realized our motorcade had been assigned a police escort. In the fifteen-year-old Mercedes Governor David Beasley and I shared, he sized up our small group and joked that if any danger were to befall us, he and I would be able to run faster than a few of the more portly members of our delegation. His wildebeest theory of security became a regular joke, but not before the exclamation point of our journey came two days later.

Beasley was a good ol' country boy whose law degree and southern charm made him an effective politician and advocate of the causes he championed. He had served four years as governor of South Carolina but had lost his reelection attempt in 1999. He attributed the end of his political career to his failed effort to remove the Confederate flag that flew above the South Carolina State House, and from this I knew him to be a man of conviction. However, he was also now a man without a constituency, so he had manufactured one: America.

That December morning in 2006, he was leading a mission to improve America's image amongst the countries most disenchanted by the United States. These were countries like Vietnam, Turkmenistan, Myanmar, Rwanda, and Yemen, the country where I would soon find myself sampling *foul* and worrying about a CNN news story.

On our second morning, the eight-member delegation assembled for breakfast in the hotel restaurant. There were surely better places to eat—the hotel's largely Western offering of omelets, fruit, and pastries was hardly authentic local cuisine, and *foul* ("fool"), a moderately spicy concoction whose principle ingredient was large, dry fava beans, was the only noteworthy local dish at the buffet. I ladled some onto my plate from the large, pear-shaped brass container in which the staple simmered. The serving utensil was odd, a flat, circular paddle that might have been good for stirring the pasty substance but was not very useful as a ladle. I remember thinking that extracting the *foul* was like playing the childhood game "Operation."

That morning, the economic officer from the US Embassy was seated next to me. A diminutive goateed man was nearby, accompanied by burly security guards. I had not yet met him but knew he was the deputy chief of mission, the US Embassy's second-in-charge. His presence was the morning's first surprise.

11

Governor Beasley requested our group's attention for what I presumed would be another of his jokes. He instead announced, in an uncharacteristically serious tone but still in his southern drawl, "It's 'bout midnight in America, so it'll be 'few hours 'fore anyone at home sees CNN. If you get any calls, you can tell your families everything's okay." I had thought the governor's jovial demeanor to be irrepressible, but something was clearly amiss. Whatever was happening, it was serious. Governor Beasley continued: "Shortly after we left last night, the Embassy was attacked. The gunman's in custody. He was shot several times, but no one at the Embassy was hurt. Right now, we think he acted alone, but the Embassy is assessing the situation. . . ."

He then offered us the opportunity to opt out of the coming week's lectures, meetings, and publicity, but I had tuned out the moment I heard that the Embassy had been attacked. It was purportedly a single gunman—his picture would be in the paper days later—but that did not matter. I could not help but think that only a few hours earlier, we had been at the US Embassy for a reception held in our honor. We were likely the target, as I learned our delegation's visit had been trumpeted days earlier by the local newspapers and our private reception at the Embassy purportedly leaked. The gunman's attack had been intended to coincide with our presence at the Embassy.

This "near miss" gave me a buzz, but it also made me pause to consider what I had gotten myself into. I was a strange character, an American businessman in Yemen, and I was beginning to love it. I was thirty-one years old and had recently published a research paper on the relationship between economic policy changes and stock market returns. Wrought with evidence, the paper presented my observation that countries experiencing an increase in economic freedom contemporaneously realize above-average stock market returns. Published in an academic journal alongside the works of three Nobel Laureates, including Milton Friedman, the paper was the basis for an investment strategy I was managing.

I was also the typical fund manager: a financial desk jockey. As a portfolio manager with two Ivy League degrees and the Chartered Financial Analyst designation, my life was much like that of my peers, characterized by hours spent in an office, analyzing investment opportunities. In the world of investment management, "hands-on" analysis generally meant holding a Wall Street Journal or tuning in to CNBC. Luckily for me, my paper was beginning to lead to unique speaking invitations, like the current one in Yemen.

My future as a portfolio manager was secure and financially rewarding. Although I was earning an income in the top one percent amongst Americans, my life felt middling. My career lacked the intrigue and excitement that I had found myself wishing for. Instead, I found excitement in other pursuits. I was deputy fire chief of a volunteer fire department, and I had been named Firefighter of the Year. I had even earned an associate's degree in firefighting science and was licensed as an emergency medical technician. Weekends and evenings were sprinkled with the excitement of medical and fire emergencies, but that made my day job as a portfolio manager that much more dreary . . . until Governor Beasley invited me to join his delegation in Yemen.

We had assembled in the hotel theater, where we would be making a full day's worth of presentations to Yemen's business leaders. I was a bit dejected upon seeing the day's schedule, as I was to speak immediately after lunch. I figured my audience might be in a food coma, as is to be expected at most symposiums held in the West. This was yet another mistaken assumption about life in Yemen: I should have been elated with the afternoon timeslot.

Fellow delegates spoke in the morning on strategic development and ethics, addressing less than fifty attendees. However, by the afternoon, more than two hundred Yemenis had arrived and listened attentively to my lecture on the virtues of free markets. Their questions were even quite poignant, once I understood them. I had been speaking in English with a sequential translation into Arabic, meaning I could say no more than two short sentences at a time lest the translator forget most of my statement. (An earlier speaker's lengthy monologues had obviously been abridged in translation.) After seeing the audience swell in size following lunch, I asked a US State Department officer for insight. He suggested that the morning's poor attendance could be related to hangovers from the previous day's *khat* sessions—though I came to doubt this much later, when I was introduced to the national *khat* addiction and found myself wide awake for two days after chewing just a few leaves of the plant. We soon learned that the morning's low turnout likely had a different culprit: Many of the Yemeni attendees had been called the previous evening and been maliciously informed that the conference had been cancelled. The plot was thickening. First gunshots, then subterfuge.

The combination of Beasley's unscripted Baptist preaching style and my empirical evidence from countries that had successfully moved from central planning to free-market economies had the effect we sought. Before the week was over, we received an unexpected invitation. We were asked to meet with the President of Yemen, Ali Abdullah Saleh. The reception was scheduled to happen near the end of our trip. First, we would travel to southern Yemen for more meetings.

Yemen holds a very important geographic position, lying at the southern tip of the Arabian Peninsula. Aden, the largest city in southern Yemen, is fortunate to be just four nautical miles from one of the world's busiest maritime shipping routes. That Somali pirates would later choose the area to ransom cargo vessels came as little surprise to me. What did surprise me was that Yemen had no coast guard at the time the USS Cole was attacked, though this had changed three years afterwards. After pointing to the site of the October 2000 Cole bombing, our Yemeni hosts were proud to identify one of their coast guard boats patrolling the harbor, one of nearly two dozen boats the United States had delivered to the Yemeni government after the tragedy. That was when I realized the importance of physical security. I had understood with sudden clarity that this was a part of the world in which people could be blown up. Never mind the challenge of untangling woefully misguided economic policies—I began emphasizing the importance of security as a precursor to foreign investment.

In Aden, we stayed in a hotel that had been built by communists when South and North Yemen were separate countries, and the south had effectively been behind an iron curtain. The country had been unified by Ali Abdullah Saleh, and we were meant to be left with no doubt of his critical role in that process when, later in the week, he awarded each of us with a Yemen Unification Medal. The medal featured Saleh carrying the Yemeni flag and was inscribed with the English words *Yemeni Unification*. His likeness was uncanny, but the French cuffs and particularly wide jacket lapels displayed on the medal were gauche.

My hotel room in Aden seemed particularly barren. Actually, I would have labeled it a deluxe suite if not for my impression that all of the units were identically sized. After all, was communism not about equality? Each had separate reception and sleeping rooms, which were overwhelming. The scale of the rooms was completely wrong. It was as if the rooms had been designed for people and furniture twice the normal size. Yet, because neither existed, the hotel proprietor had made due with IKEA and mortals. I presumed the hotel had been a retreat of Soviet Union officials, perhaps of the Eastern European vintage.

Just as I had observed when my plane landed with another round of applause in Aden, most everything seemed quite different than in America, even the shape of the soda cans. They were tall, skinny eight-ounce cans with pull-tab tops that constantly reminded me that I was not in a developed Western economy. An odd sticker affixed to the bureau in my hotel room would have been an enigma had I not seen something similar on the plane. There were no words on the sticker, just a large arrow pointing at an odd angle across the room. I had seen the same thing displayed on the overhead screens of the plane several times during the flight. This was the direction of Mecca.

The former President of Yemen, Ali Abdullah Saleh, and the author

Yemeni political leaders of the time claimed to want to liberalize Yemen's economy to attract investment and to witness the resultant economic growth. Yet, several months later, we learned their enthusiasm had waned. Like a junkie, I found myself experiencing withdrawal. I continued my desk job, managing portfolios of stock investments, but I could not forget my intense introduction to Yemen and to Arab culture. The experience had given me a new desire to work in a country transitioning from a centrally planned communist economy to free-market capitalism. I had expressed my dream to Howie over tea but was left without much hope I would find the opportunity I sought. So when Howie called and asked me to fly to Egypt, I jumped at the opportunity. First, though, he had to explain the project to me.

He asked if I knew about rent-controlled real estate. I did not. He explained the important facts: A populist government panders to voters by preventing rents from rising. After several years, tenants are paying much less rent than they otherwise should. This makes for lost income to the landlord and significantly lessens the value of an apartment building. By the time our conversation ended, I had agreed to travel to Egypt within the month.

He forwarded a nearly inch-thick dossier of every email exchange he'd had with a lawyer, a business consultant, and two real estate brokers, all of whom were Egyptian. This would give me a crash course on Egyptian rent control. Then I was to offer my on-the-ground opinion of the urban Cairo real estate investment market. My objective was to determine whether Howie's thirty years of success as a redeveloper of New York City rent control properties could be replicated in Cairo.

Having read the emails, I thought Howie must have been quite eager. Paying rent-control tenants to abandon their units was legal in Egypt, and there was no shortage of rent-controlled properties. Almost every property in Egypt was rent controlled. Yet, in the dossier of emails, there was also a measure of disconnect. The Egyptians with whom Howie was corresponding did not seem to "get it." Their written responses to Howie's questions indicated doubt as to why anyone would want to buy neglected buildings that produced no rental income unless the intent was to demolish and replace them with skyscrapers. No one had ever endeavored to redevelop the rent-controlled belle époque buildings of Downtown, a bustling borough of Cairo.

In his late sixties, Howie was looking for a fresh rent control market, one that presented the same opportunity he had seen in the 1960s in New York City. He wanted a city full of neglected rent-controlled buildings that could be renovated and remarketed at higher prices once most of the tenants had been paid to leave. In his search, Howie wrote letters to free-market activists around the world. He only wanted to know if rent control existed in their countries. The meagerness of the responses gave him little hope of finding the jewel, as he saw it, of an untouched rent-control market. Then he had a chance meeting in Canada.

Howie explained to me that he had become acquainted with an economic development consultant at a cocktail reception. The consultant had just been in Cairo and had a topical understanding of the Egyptian rent-control market. The difference between free-market and rent-control prices in Cairo was purportedly gigantic.

Four more trips to Cairo and two years of due diligence followed. I could sense there was an opportunity to have the fix I had been seeking since Yemen. Convincing financial partners of the opportunity in Cairo was difficult, as potential investors knew the financial crisis had been exacerbated by the illiquidity of certain investments. We were asking investors to make a particularly illiquid investment, one that could last up to eight years. We made two key commitments that enabled us to secure investment capital when most others were having serious difficulty raising funds in the post-financial crisis environment. First, Howie committed twenty percent of the capital, making him very interested in the partnership's overall success. Second, I was going to be closely involved with the operations in Egypt. One investor even demanded to be released from his investment if a bad fate befell both Howie and me. He had no such stipulation regarding the involvement of any of our Egyptian colleagues, and that signaled to us that having an Egyptian executive participate in our local operations was not critical to obtaining investors.

We eventually raised enough money to start our endeavor, and I was about to be the first foreign direct investor to step off the airplane with a suitcase full of cash in a country that, only five years earlier, had been ranked amongst the top ten percent of countries in which it was most difficult to conduct business. I hoped that I could live up to the expectations of our investors and my American partner. Howie did not suffer fools.

3 LIBERALIZING THE LEGACY

Egyptian politics in one sentence: Nasser turned left,
Sadat turned right, and Mubarak stayed in the
middle, going nowhere for thirty years.

Gamal Abdel Nasser was a photogenic colonel in the Egyptian Army who, in 1952, led a revolution to overthrow the monarchy. Although a significant departure from Egyptian policy at the time, his purported principle of uniting workers against an autocracy was not revolutionary when viewed in historical context. His methods were de rigueur in a time when communist revolutions were afoot: Ho Chi Minh's communists removed the French colonialists from Vietnam in 1945, Kim Il-Sung declared Korea to be a communist state in 1948, and Fidel Castro led an armed conflict in 1953, resulting in a communist coup of the Cuban state.

Like his revolutionary peers, Nasser was also a redistributionist. He had unfettered access to tremendous wealth and to the productive industry of the Jewish community, aristocratic Egyptians, and foreigners, many of whom were abandoning Egypt in droves. Companies, buildings, and even the Suez Canal were nationalized. This was a history I could not ignore, as I represented foreign direct investors in a niche property market that had been partly nationalized by the Nasser administration. Approximately thirty percent of the market we targeted remained the property of state-owned enterprises. Though we declared nationalized properties off-limits, we still found plenty of buildings for sale.

Thirteen years after the Suez Canal opened, British forces defeated the Egyptian Army to begin their occupation of the country in 1882. Under the colonialists' rule, a seven-decade economic boom resulted in the construction of more than five hundred belle époque–era buildings in the Downtown borough of Cairo alone. With architecture that could cause visitors to easily mistake any of the streets that fed into Tahrir Square for Paris' Avenue des Champs-Élysées, Downtown became the focus of our investment efforts.

With enough privately owned properties for sale, I found there was good reason to avoid buildings that had been nationalized, as reparations claims by exiled Jewish Egyptians were becoming increasingly frequent, and, in one noteworthy case, such a claim proved successful. The Cecil Hotel was Alexandria's most famous lodging. Built in 1929 by the French-Egyptian Jewish Metzger family, the hotel had served as quarters for Winston Churchill, Al Capone, and, reportedly, the British Secret Service. In 2007, after a lengthy court battle, the hotel was returned to the Metzger family, who immediately sold it to the Egyptian government. The last risk I wanted to take was to buy a property that could be declared stolen, as was eventually the case with the Cecil Hotel. (For tourism purposes, the hotel is now managed by Sofitel and is worthy of a visit.)

My admittedly simplistic view was that Nasser's communist nationalizations and socialist redistributions had worked because he had an endowment: a vibrant, reasonably free market and worldly economy that preceded his ascension to power. Over time, the metaphorical pie of economic wealth became smaller as redistribution fueled consumption and Nasser's populism stifled economic investment and growth. During Sadat's tenure, Margaret Thatcher said, "The problem with socialism is that you eventually run out of other people's money." As such, by the time Mubarak was deposed, all that remained were crumbs, much like the crumbling buildings of Downtown.

Downtown's architecture: 7 Abd El Salam Aref Street

Following Nasser's death in 1970, his vice president, Anwar Sadat, assumed the presidency of Egypt. Though awarded the Nobel Peace Prize, Sadat was almost universally hated in the Arab world for signing the Camp David peace treaty with Israel. However, he also made significant fiscal contributions to Egyptian policy. Aiming to stimulate growth and productivity through private-sector investment, he reversed course from Nasser's socialist policies towards policies of economic liberalization. This meant that the strained government budget would need to be repaired by lifting price controls on basic necessities.

Sadat was met with a series of riots protesting the increased price of bread. The massive riots lasted for two days and were responsible for 120 buses and hundreds of buildings being destroyed in Cairo alone, and they ended with the reinstitution of subsidies and price controls.

Sadat's free-market "open door" policy to investors read well as a headline and was welcomed by Western governments still fighting the Cold War. Yet not much substantive progress was made by Sadat or his successor, Hosni Mubarak. Mubarak did little to address the economic challenges Egypt faced or to improve the country's attractiveness to foreign investors. This stagnation continued until his son, Gamal Mubarak, was appointed leader of the legislative committee in 2004 and took over management of economic policy. Egypt desperately needed radical changes to its economic policy—fifty years after the Nasser revolution, it had become one of the most difficult countries in which to conduct business.

Ranking near the bottom of a list of countries evaluated by the World Bank in 2004, Egypt was a terrible environment for investors. Reports on bureaucratic interference and delay identified several factors that made registering a new business in Egypt exceptionally burdensome: These included the process of securing permits and complying with tax policy. What little was left of Egypt's economic pie was insufficient to meet the now decades-long redistributionist patterns of the government. Egypt had a structural budget deficit and a chronic overspending problem.

By 2007, the Egyptian government had passed a number of laws that made the investment environment more hospitable: The top tax bracket was lowered from forty-two percent to twenty percent, the fee to register property was lowered from three percent of the property's value to a flat sum of $350, commercial courts were created to expedite contractual disputes, and procedures for starting a business were greatly simplified. Accolades followed, with the International Finance Corporation noting, "In 2006/07 Egypt tops the list of reformers that are making it easier to do business. Egypt's reforms went deep . . . [and it] greatly improved its position in the global rankings as a result." *The Wall Street Journal's* ranking of economic freedom explained, "According to our 2008 assessment . . . [Egypt's] overall score is 4 percentage points higher than last year, the largest improvement of any country. Improvements in business, financial, and trade freedom were significant."

While Egyptian legislators and Gamal Mubarak, the architect of economic liberalization, captured headlines, cronies of the Mubarak regime took advantage of certain structural changes to the economy. More than fifty years after Nasser's socialist revolution, the Egyptian government held a plethora of assets. State-owned companies, banks, and empty land were national treasures but held little value, as they had been inefficiently used. Some operated at losses, and, as the government needed funds, it recognized that its function was not to serve as a manager of businesses or custodian of fallow land.

Thus, in the late 1990s, under a new privatization program, the government began to sell its assets to private owners. A beer brewer, a department store, banks, and an agricultural seed company were just some of the assets sold in various auctions. Prime undeveloped land was also auctioned by the government, and the seemingly below-market prices paid would be the basis for corruption allegations and numerous lawsuits that predated the 2011 uprising but multiplied in the post-Mubarak period. Whether the prices paid were fair required a case-by-case assessment. Many companies were losing money but held valuable assets, such as tracts of land. Other companies were privatized with the condition that employees could not be fired, greatly restricting the investors' flexibility and warranting a steep discount on the price paid to acquire the company. However, the fact remained that a number of the investors who had purchased privatized assets were close associates of the Mubarak family.

Owners of privatized companies began to expect greater productivity from workers than had been expected by government managers. An acquaintance of mine, who was a privatized bank executive, explained that he had been forbidden to fire employees hired by the government prior to privatization. In an attempt to solve the problem, his team had hired new bank staff and paid them much more than the government workers were earning. Government-hired employees, if incompetent, were kept at their low salary levels and were asked not to do anything but show up to work, lest they interfere with the productive new hires, and those who objected were sent to the miserable work environments of Upper Egypt. The hope, my acquaintance explained, was that the malcontent employees would resign.

A few owners of previously state-owned businesses failed to fulfill commitments related to the privatizations. Omar Effendi was a national department store chain founded in 1856 and nationalized in 1957. In 2006, the chain was privatized and sold to a Saudi Arabian investor, who secured funding from the International Finance Corporation, an entity associated with the World Bank. According to one report, "[The Saudi owner] failed to pay wages on time . . . refused to pay suppliers . . . and some of the major stores . . . are barely functioning." Before Egypt's January 2011 uprising, lawsuits had already been filed by activist lawyers, demanding that the privatizations be overturned and the companies returned to state ownership. Three months after Hosni Mubarak resigned, Omar Effendi was renationalized.

The mismanagement of privatized businesses stirred discontent, but the Mubarak regime largely ignored it. There were privatization success stories like that of Al-Ahram Beverage Corporation (ABC), the maker of Egypt's national beer, which deflected criticism. The United States Agency for International Development credited the success to management changes: "ABC's management style was restructured in a manner where it would be consumer, rather than production, oriented. . . . The taste of ABC's product both improved noticeably and was standardized at the quality control level in a short period of time. The company's fleet of trucks was expanded and upgraded and the numbers of its distribution outlets jumped from

10,000 to 45,000 nationwide."[1] However, the obscene profits made by Mubarak's cronies brought tempers to a boil.

I had never seen a Mercedes-Benz Maybach car in person, even in the posh neighborhoods of Kensington and Mayfair, London. They were luxury sedans whose price tag of more than $400 thousand meant only a handful could afford them. In 2010, only 157 were sold.[2] Fortune magazine panned the car, describing it as "an inferior automobile wrapped in a glitzy package."[3] The article continued, "Maybach strived for a prestige that it tried to ground on price alone. The wealthy figured it out in a hurry and stayed away in droves. Appearances to the contrary sometimes notwithstanding, the top 0.0001% didn't accumulate all that money by being stupid."

So when I saw a metallic royal blue Maybach parked outside the chichi Cairo restaurant Apperitivo, I inspected it closely. The stately car was exceptionally long and its color flashy. The tan leather interior must have required a herd of cattle to produce. What caught my eye were the initials EZZ, which were embroidered in the headrests. I thought the owner must have had a weird name if two of the initials were Z. This was eight weeks before the January 25, 2011, uprising, only after which I discovered the car's owner had not made his money by being stupid. No, he had wisely made his money from government decisions that effectively gave him a monopoly over steel production.

Prior to the Egyptian uprising, Ahmed Ezz had served as a National Democratic Party (NDP) member of parliament and was chairman of the budget committee. He was also chairman of a steel

---

[1] United States Agency for International Development, Privatization Coordination Support Unit, "The Post Privatization Development of Former Law 203 Companies," June 2000, p. 9. Retrieved from http://www.scribd.com/doc/52894038/6/Al-Ahram-Beverages-Company-ABC.

[2] Alex Taylor III, "Mercedes puts Maybach out of its misery," *CNNMoney*, November 28, 2011. Retrieved from http://money.cnn.com/2011/11/28/autos/maybach_mercedes_shut_down.fortune.

[3] Ibid.

company that held more than sixty percent of the market share. Egyptian anti-monopoly legislation partly defined the existence of a monopoly as being when a company held more than a twenty-five percent market share, but other factors were also used in determining the existence of a monopoly, such as a producer's influence over prices and suppliers. Ezz Steel was repeatedly accused of being a monopoly, though it never received an adverse court verdict. A 2009 business publication of the American University in Cairo declared,

> *Unexpectedly, the investigations concluded in January 2009 that Ezz Steel has not violated . . . Law No.3 of 2005. . . . Ahmed Ezz is not only being criticized because of increasing steel prices but also because of the exaggerated privileges he receives. His favorable position in the NDP and his highly connected social and political network have facilitated his business transactions and discriminated against other market players. . . . Ezz was provided with loans. . . . Other facilities favoring Ahmed Ezz include subsidized energy and other services like Al Dekheila seaport and a gas line costing EGP 160 million (US$ 26.7 million). Yet these privileges never trickle down to end consumers in the form of lower prices. . . . The question that arises is whether the government is turning a blind eye on Ahmed Ezz's operations.[4]*

The article concluded with a sentiment that had existed in the few years prior to the uprising. The government was actively working to liberalize the economy while simultaneously affording special privileges to certain businesses:

---

[4] Zeinab Abdallah, "Steel Market in Egypt: A Case of Power Abuse?" *The Chronicles*, Fall 2009, p. 19–23. Retrieved from http://www.aucegypt.edu/research/ebhrc/publications/Documents/Steel%20Market%20in%20Egypt.pdf.

We are left to wonder whose side the law is taking, the side of the end consumers or that of monopolistic practices in the market. . . . If the Egyptian government is willing to take active steps to promote fair competition among all producers then why does it continue to turn a blind eye to Ahmed Ezz and many other dominant producers in other sectors that are restricting free market practices?

The market liberalizations were attracting praise from multilateral financial institutions and drawing foreign direct investors to Egypt. However, those free-market policy changes would soon be mistaken for the crony capitalism that was simultaneously afoot in Egypt. The trickle-down effects of economic liberalization were nonetheless evident. For one, salaries of college graduates were increasing. However, the trickling did not overcome occasionally ostentatious displays of wealth by the nouveau riche, and the royal blue Maybach was the pièce de résistance.

That same night, I also saw the lemon man, who was a fixture of Cairo nightlife. He always donned a brown galabeya, the traditional full-length, dress-like garment that rural Egyptian men wore. He was a poor man from the country, though, judging by his height and girth, I did not think he ever went hungry. He stood hunched, supporting himself with a wooden cane whose accumulated wear suggested it was a necessity, not a stage prop. His shoeless, soiled feet suggested a hard life. I imagined he had spent years walking the fertile fields along the Nile.

The lemon man would arrive at about nine at night with a dozen or more small bags of lemons. The citrus fruits were green and looked more like undersized limes. He offered them for sale to everyone leaving Apperitivo. The going rate was five Egyptian pounds, less than one American dollar, for a dozen small lemons.

I had never really known what to do with a bag of so many lemons. Their juice is used as a condiment to soups and chicken dishes in Egypt, and my office manager recommended I drink warm water with lemon juice whenever I was sick. The tonic always helped, but the few lemons in my refrigerator had nevertheless hardened into jawbreaker-sized fossils. I rarely had use for them, so I never bought a bag of lemons from the lemon man. Instead, I occasionally gave him the one or two Egyptian pounds floating around in my pocket. He was particularly polite when he solicited any passersby to buy a bag of lemons. For those who declined, he always responded with an Eyah haga, meaning any money would be fine. I suspected he made more money as a beggar than a fruit vendor, but he looked to need the donations much more than any beggar I had seen in the West, where, in my hometown of Boston, I had seen panhandlers listening to MP3 players and propelled by expensive motorized wheelchairs.

That particular evening, the Mercedes Maybach was juxtaposed with the lemon man. It was a telling sign that the new wealth may not have been trickling down fast enough. While the World Bank lauded the Mubarak regime for making genuine reforms, certain cronies of the regime were still being awarded privileges. For market liberalizations to be accepted, wealth needed to trickle down more quickly, and there could be no privileged cronies, subsidized industrial inputs, or protected markets such as that of Ahmed Ezz. A regular chant during the Egyptian uprising was for social justice, and in some ways, the uprising achieved it: In October of 2012, Ahmed Ezz was convicted of money laundering and was sentenced to seven years in jail, along with a $3-billion fine.

4 BUSINESS BEGINS

In Cairo, I counted writers, photojournalists, and foreign aid staffers as friends. Also among my circle were CEOs, economists, engineers, and diplomats, most of whom were or had been expatriates. Even quite a few of my Egyptian friends had lived outside the country at some point. Learning about my friends' cultural experiences, like observing the sport of Buzkashi, intrigued me.

Wendy Steavenson had been part of my visceral experience in Tahrir Square during the November 2011 Mohammed Mahmoud Street violence. In a more relaxed setting, that of a dinner party, she explained the Afghani sport to me. She had witnessed it firsthand. It sounded like rugby played on horseback while en route to a slaughterhouse. Then I saw the pictures of a match, which Max Becherer, a Cairo-based freelance photographer, had captured.

Max was a photojournalist who had worked for several years at the Baghdad bureau of *The New York Times*. In Cairo, he captured some of the most descriptive images of the Egyptian uprising. His body of work included cover photos for *Time Magazine* and *The New York Times*, but amongst his friends and in only one late-night instance I had witnessed, he was Elvis. His well-travelled but immaculate sequined jumpsuit and skillful hip shakes must have given his friends much-needed relief to the stress of living in the places he had called home.

His photos evidenced what Wendy had explained of Buzkashi. Teams had at least ten riders each, and the "ball" was a headless goat or calf carcass. The spectacle looked to be the stomping ground of great equestrians: Some players held the reins by their teeth, which freed both arms to grapple for the animal corpse.

Wendy and Max were in Cairo to document history. My reason for being in Cairo was more complicated. Though the question always came up at social gatherings, I had difficulty explaining my job. For one, "job" was a misnomer. I was a partner, a self-employed business manager. "Hedge fund manager," even though an accurate description, conjured up images of a Wall Street desk jockey, which was hardly how I saw myself. I usually responded, "I manage some Egyptian companies for American investors. What we're doing is trying to buy and restore some of the beautiful old buildings in Downtown." Everyone loved the idea, but some knew to ask of the major obstacle: rent control.

The first instance of rent control in Egypt was in the 1920s, when pith helmets and monocles were de rigueur, though the legislation pertinent to our real estate work was passed in 1944, when rent control was expanded to include all rental properties. Legislators aimed to protect existing renters from rapidly increasing rents while also encouraging the construction of additional rental properties by exempting properties built after 1944. A decade later, rents on post-1944 properties were escalating rapidly. New legislation during the years 1952–1965 reduced rents in existing rent-controlled units and extended rent controls to include newly constructed, post-1944 buildings. The only rent-control exemption which then remained was on furnished luxury units, whose high rents meant such apartments were usually tenanted by foreigners.

Rent-control policies were a scourge that left no one content. In Egypt, residential rents were legislated to escalate by one percent annually. Inflation, however, averaged fifteen percent per year, and this meant the purchasing power of a landlord's rental income decreased by fourteen percent every year. This effect compounded over more than sixty years, leaving rent-controlled apartment dwellers paying two dollars in rent per month while a free-market equivalent rent could be five hundred to one thousand times higher, at between one and two thousand dollars per month.

The huge discrepancy between what landlords should have earned and what tenants actually paid caused problems and distorted the property market. One of the obvious effects, visible to even the casual observer, was neglected building maintenance. Common areas—the elevator, stairwells, and exterior—were rarely maintained by the building owner because repair costs easily exceeded income.

In the building where I lived, there were four cisterns on the roof. Water was stored above the building to increase water pressure in the higher floors. My building was eight stories tall, though Egyptians, as do Europeans, label the first elevated floor as the first floor. The street-level floor in Egypt was called *idoor el ard*—literally, "floor of the ground." In Cairo's many French-manufactured elevators, the button labeled RC, for *rez-de-chaussée*, would leave you at street level.

In my second-floor apartment, I noticed the cisterns failed at another purpose: storing water. Water service seemed to be interrupted almost weekly, with outages usually lasting half a day. The cisterns should have supplied enough water until municipal service was restored, but the rent-control laws had led to an endemic neglect of building repairs, meaning that three of our four cisterns barely held any water. Their walls had been perforated by rust, the repair long neglected.

The allocation of repair costs to tenants was a constant source of tension, as repairs could only be completed when residents became organized. These resident unions were made up of rent-control tenants, who effectively owned their apartments, and landlords who collected normal market rent. Apartment owners who were burdened by rent-controlled tenants were not expected to contribute to a building's general maintenance.

Repair cost allocation was usually determined by a tenant's number of apartments or his total square footage. If a particular tenant disagreed with the necessity of a repair or could not afford it, he or she would simply not contribute funds, and those who funded repairs were always left paying more than their fair share. This had obvious repercussions. On occasion, I would visit buildings where the elevators were accessed by keys or modified to bypass certain floors—this was explained as a method of restricting use of the elevator to those who contributed to its maintenance.

When tenants ran out of patience for their tenant unions, they sometimes took matters into their own hands. Months before I arrived, my neighbor had requested that a secure door be installed at the building's entrance, but she had been waiting for a reply and decided to work around the problem. The banging lasted but one full day, and by the time the metal smiths had finished, a cage had been installed around the entrance to my neighbor's apartment. The structure resembled a ceiling-high animal pen behind which she could open her apartment door and safely view who was in the hallway. When her keys banged against the ironwork every morning as she opened the door, I would remark to my office manager that the zoo was opening for business.

Another consequence of Egypt's rent controls was that building ownership had become diluted, sometimes dramatically so. For many decades there had been no willing buyers of rent-controlled buildings, as such buildings produced almost no income. Likewise, the tenants were often difficult to manage, and eviction was rare. For these reasons, ownership interests in buildings initially owned by one or two landlords had been distributed to numerous descendants during several successive inheritances. One well-known six-building parcel had almost ninety owners, and its prime location across the street from the headquarters of the Central Bank of Egypt meant we examined it closely as an acquisition candidate. Our due diligence on the property revealed that ownership had remained within one family since 1908. That was when I also learned about Muslim inheritance rules, which were completely different than anything I knew in the West.

In Egypt, inheritance is governed by the intricate laws of Islam regardless of one's religion. There, a male inheritor's share is twice that of a female inheritor. As well, legitimate inheritors are not only the spouse and children but also parents, brothers, sisters, and male grandchildren of the deceased. With so many interests, building ownership could quickly become divided, leaving most rent-controlled properties held by many minority owners. One solution was to subdivide the building. However, use and even ownership of a specific apartment was sometimes allocated to a minority owner when his or her ownership percentage was at least the same as that of the apartment's square footage ratio in the building. When ownership became too diluted to allocate apartments, one minority owner would inevitably collect and proportionally distribute rental income to these passive owners.

Rent control had not only limited the transfer of building ownership to inheritances but had also led to inefficient housing solutions. Most owners had acquired their ownership interests through inheritance, and they preferred money to an ownership interest in a building with little income. When an apartment became empty, the apartment was sometimes sold, and proceeds were allocated to the owners of the building. Selling an apartment, though, was problematic in the long run. The terms of Egyptian law made it difficult to transfer a building's title without the accession of individual apartment owners.

This potential headache may have been the impetus for fifty-nine-year leases, for which incoming tenants would pay a lump sum upon signing the rent contract. The tenant would then make nearly immaterial monthly payments for fifty-nine years. This duration was chosen because an untested Egyptian law prohibited leases from lasting more than sixty years. We contemplated filing a test case to determine whether the legislation applied to aged rent-control contracts, but the thought of going to court was fleeting. With nominal litigation costs in Egypt, both parties to a dispute generally exhausted all appeals, which could take up to seven years, longer than our business model allowed. We also suspected that using litigation to evict tenants might attract frivolous quid pro quo lawsuits aimed to delay us.

In 1981, the Egyptian government had attempted to formalize the rental market by legislating behaviors that had arisen in the absence of free-market rental transactions. The tenant's right to pay rent much less than the free-market rate was valuable, so the foremost issue in the legislation was determining how rent-control contracts could be transferred. The lump sum amount paid by an incoming tenant to assume the below-market rent contract was to be split, with half paid to the outgoing tenant and half to the building's owner. The landlord could deny the transfer of a rent-control contract but rarely did so unless the tenant was illegal or about to die, thereby freeing the apartment to be sold. A lump sum payment was too attractive to owners after years of collecting little in the way of rental income.

Shops were also rent controlled, though shop tenants preferred to transfer their businesses along with the rent contracts. In this case, "transfer" was a figurative description, as the outgoing shopkeeper would become a silent partner in his business by taking on the incoming store tenant as a business partner. Of course, the outgoing shopkeeper would receive a payment for the concession of the business and, more importantly, the rent-controlled lease. This allowed both tenants to avoid paying the landlord the legislated fifty percent of the fee, as the outgoing shop tenant would never be removed as an owner in this scheme.

There were three circumstances in which a rent-control contract could be ended. The least likely situation was one in which when a rent-control tenant voluntarily vacated his or her unit. However, with indefinite inheritability, it seemed that heirs always moved in with aging tenants, meaning units were always inhabited. The second most likely situation was one in which the landlord paid the tenant a lump sum to leave. This amount was labeled key money and was legal in Egypt. Yet, after decades of rent control and socialist governments, most Egyptian landlords had little money to pay tenants to leave. As well, landlords I spoke to were afraid that if they invested to empty their buildings of tenants, rent-control policies might worsen.

Rather than wait for death or pay a tenant key money, landlords most frequently relied on coercion to empty rent-controlled units. They would file lawsuits, designing legal proceedings merely to harass a tenant. Other landlords would claim a tenant to be in contractual violation, such as the failure to pay rent. However, although a verdict declaring the rent unpaid might cost the tenant legal fees to mount his defense, he could usually remedy the situation by simply paying the overdue rent with interest. Tenants had become wise to this coercion. For example, a rent-control tenant would often pay a year's worth of rent at the police station, where the police would notarize the receipt of rent and a court bailiff would later deliver the rent to the landlord. The process was a horrible waste of time and government resources.

Worse were the landlords who inconvenienced or threatened tenants. Elevators were shut down for extended periods, reportedly for maintenance, and water leaks were also arranged to inconvenience tenants. The most gruesome tactic, though, was explained to me with a straight face. In a due diligence meeting with one of Egypt's most renowned lawyers, I inquired about the availability of property insurance. With the economics of rent-controlled buildings at the time, I should not have been surprised to learn that few buildings in Cairo were insured. Landlords could not use the building or collect much in the way of rent, and the buildings were like old heirlooms left in an attic, largely forgotten.

The lawyer shocked me when he told me to forget about insuring the building. Rather, he suggested I should hope for any building I owned to collapse. He explained that owners gain immensely from the collapse of a building. In such an event, tenant contracts are all voided, and the landlord can rebuild, offering new market-rate contracts at much higher rents. I noted that this phenomenon happened with great frequency in Alexandria. In a twelve-month period from January 2012 to 2013, there were at least seven building collapses that killed more than sixty people.

Most collapsed buildings had been condemned years earlier, the government having authorized demolition. At the time, 111 thousand buildings were subject to demolition orders in Egypt, and in demolition lay an opportunity for landlords to recover their wealth. Demolition was just cause to evict tenants without payment of key money, and in some instances, landlords bribed bureaucrats to issue demolition orders. I even bid on three buildings whose principle selling point, according to the owners, was that their neglected condition would allow me to obtain a demolition permit and evict tenants. In these cases, we judged the buildings salvageable.

The ruse had been exposed years before our endeavor, the result being that tenants delayed eviction for a year or sometimes longer by claiming that demolition orders had been procured illegally. Because of this, buildings that had been rightly condemned regularly collapsed while tenants were inside. Though some condemned buildings had been illegally constructed, others were damaged rent-controlled properties. In some measure, the resultant deaths from building collapses can be attributed to the rent-control policy.

Politicians worldwide now recognize the negative effects of rent control. Policies meant to control housing prices not only led to the neglect of buildings but also discouraged the construction of new supply, creating a shortage of housing. *Yacoubian Building* was a 2006 blockbuster film in Egypt that depicted the daily lives of tenants in an Egyptian rent-controlled property. True of many buildings in Cairo, families inhabit the rooftop of the Yacoubian Building. Originally designed as storerooms or washrooms, rooftop structures have become homes for those affected by the housing shortage. The most striking example of rooftop housing I knew was atop three adjoining buildings on a prestigious street in the Heliopolis borough of Cairo. I had considered buying the buildings with a combined footprint of

1,480 square meters, only to discover that approximately thirty families resided on the roof.

The Egyptian government recognized the social perversions, neglected building stock, and pervasive housing shortages that came from the policy of rent control. So, in 1996, the government addressed the indefinite inheritability of a rent-control contract by limiting inheritance to one subsequent generation. Why not summarily end rent controls? While rent-control tenants are a large political constituency, landlords are not. This meant that immediate removal of rent controls was unlikely, as doing so would be political suicide. Ending rent-control contracts upon the death of the second-generation tenant meant the end of rent control would come about in the distant future. It was politically clever.

We expected rent-controlled buildings to be quite inexpensive. Our market inquiries suggested a rent-controlled square foot could be had for about twenty-three to twenty-five dollars. Once we acquired the building, we would pay tenants a similar amount to leave. In the case of a 125-square-meter apartment, key money would be about five times Egypt's per-capita GDP. However, things in Egypt never went as I expected. In every building negotiation, sellers' asking prices were many times higher than what could be justified by economic reality. This was when business would really begin, when I learned to negotiate like an Egyptian. First, though, I needed to learn how to palm money like one.

5 TEA MONEY

In the Middle East, personal space is violable. I inevitably found that others stood uncomfortably close to me while waiting in line, and an American expatriate friend even took to telling anyone who stood too close to step back or buy him a cocktail. However, I eventually grew accustomed to having much less personal space. What I never did become accustomed to was holding hands with a man in public.

I was the product of a military boarding school where public displays of affection were forbidden. Holding hands was tolerable, but it was also my most permissible intimacy. Perhaps for this reason, I rarely hold hands with even my wife to this day, save to comfort her during the few nerve-rattling seconds during an airplane landing. Two heterosexual men holding hands in the West is unheard of, so imagine my complete surprise when an Egyptian police officer casually grabbed my hand in public, as if we were a couple of love-struck teens. As my hand grew immediately slippery with sweat, he must have noticed my discomfort, yet he continued to firmly hold it. He had a plan.

My time in Yemen had made me aware that Arab men sometimes hold hands while walking, yet I had not observed this behavior in Egypt during my first trip to Cairo. What would have made for a faux pas in the West was once again another example of how exactly opposite life can be amongst Arabs.

I noticed the police officer was armed with an AK-47. Slung casually over his shoulder, his gun was identical to those I would later see carried by the Egyptian policeman who guarded all embassy perimeters. Those armed civil servants were mostly teenage boys from rural Upper Egypt, and I saw them several times a day, most often stationed in front of the Algerian embassy within blocks of my office. They were colorful and hardly intimidating, but I noted that following the January 25 uprising, they usually disappeared at the first sign of unrest. This was particularly true for those who guarded the US Embassy.

Though they had several stations posted some distance apart around an embassy, much of the time I found them huddled around a single telephone booth–sized post. The monotony of their duty was sometimes broken by Egyptian music played from the speaker of a cell phone, the electrical charge maintained for the duration of their shift by illegally tapping into the wires of a nearby streetlamp.

I had discretely studied their weapons every time I passed an embassy. Their AK-47s were so old that much of the anodized coloring had worn from the metal parts, and the gunstocks' wood was often deeply scarred. I had been told that these policemen had not been issued ammunition, but I was never certain. More frightening was the idea that the Egyptian government might not trust its own police force with ammunition.

I had just finished dining alone at the InterContinental hotel, which overlooked the Nile, and was returning to my hotel several blocks away. During my ten-day research trips to Cairo, I had not yet perfected the hardly pedestrian art of crossing a street. The technique involves stopping between lanes and awaiting a break in traffic while cars pass within inches both in front and behind. This particular evening, I had stopped in the raised median of the Qasr El Nil Bridge, next to where a young policeman was standing. Having seen that I was a clean-shaven, suited foreigner, he must have felt I was too patient in waiting for traffic to pass. He quickly grabbed my hand and, with a sufficiently strong grip to prevent me from removing mine, stepped out in front of the traffic he had halted with his raised opposite hand.

After having safely crossed, I thanked him in Arabic. I continued on the sidewalk, and so too did he, right alongside me. He began asking me questions: Where was I from, where was I going, and what was my name? I answered with the few words of Arabic I knew at that point. As we walked, I felt he might either escort me the full distance to my hotel or find one of my answers sufficiently objectionable to take me to his leader. In either case, I was not fond of having an AK-47, loaded or not, astride me. When I slipped free of his grasp, I inserted both of my hands into my pockets. I figured that was likely to prevent him from again taking me by the hand, and I felt a few Egyptian pound notes wadded up in my pocket.

Casual service providers in Egypt work for small tips. This *baksheesh*, loosely translated as "tips" and sometimes called "tea money," is expected by porters, grocery baggers, and even the policeman who overlooks your double-parked car. If one fails to pay the usual one- to five-pound tip, one might hear the word baksheesh mentioned. So, before going out for dinner that evening, I had stuffed several five-pound notes in my front pocket. Figuring the policeman was looking for a tip, I pulled out a fiver and discreetly palmed it to him. He expertly accepted the folded bill in a manner much as I had seen drug deals depicted on any television crime drama. Though the amount was less than one US dollar, this was the first time in my life that I had ever tipped a government official, and it would be only one of many such instances. The amounts were rarely more than several multiples of what I had slipped Mohamed that evening. (Yes, I asked his name, too.)

Another vivid example came two years later, shortly after the 2011 uprising. I was finalizing the formation of a new Egyptian company at the Office of Social Insurance, where I gave proof that I was the chairman of the new company and provided my signature for the ministerial records. To complete these bureaucratic social insurance formalities, my accountant, Samer Talaat Hanna, assigned one of his junior accountants to take me to the backroom of a government building.

Samer had the perfect personality to offset the maddening Egyptian bureaucracy. He managed to finish most sentences with a laugh and a smile that was amplified by his modest overbite. He had inherited the habit from his father, Talaat Ibrahim Hanna, who managed their accounting firm. I figured their good humor had been responsible for much of their success helping clients navigate Egypt's byzantine business regulations. That skill was matched by their professional image. Never did I see Samer or his father in anything but a suit and tie during working hours, even on the hottest of Cairo's summer days, when temperatures rose to the mid-nineties for weeks in a row.

Samer must have known the scene I would find at the government office and opted to avoid it by sending his colleague. In that room, I found five male employees hovering around one of five desks. Two women sat at other desks. The men were smoking, drinking tea, and fighting over a bureaucratic procedure. There was a single antiquated computer, one older than I ever remember using, and vertical files were overly stuffed with papers, all seemingly important signature cards like one I would need to complete that day. File drawers were partially closed, blocked by completed forms not full inserted. The overcrowding of the file drawers was much like that found in the housing situation around greater Cairo, where people lived in graveyards and building utility rooms.

I greeted the room in Arabic with the customary "Peace be upon you all." As my accountant's colleague explained to one of the men what we needed to accomplish, we were directed to an older woman in the room. She held the blank signature cards—and an interest in America. With remarkable frequency, my introductory conversations with Egyptian bureaucrats, taxi drivers, and other workers followed the same pattern:

Her: Where are you from?

Me: I'm from America but live in Zamalek [a wealthy Cairo borough].

Her: How long have you lived in Egypt?

Me: One year.

Her: You speak Arabic well. Do you love Egypt?

Me: Yes, I love the weather. Egyptian people are good. Would you like some chocolates? I just bought these.

While I was befriending the woman, who seemed to have a management role, the junior accountant advocated for me during a loud exchange with one of the men who had been reviewing our corporate documents in the office. He won the day by emphasizing that foreign businessmen like me would leave Egypt if bureaucrats insisted on following stupid procedures. Moments later, I would be allowed to complete the social insurance office's signature card.

A couple of weeks had passed when Samer returned to the same social insurance office to halt our tax obligations on a resigned employee. He returned from his visit to report that we could not remove an employee from the social insurance rolls until a replacement employee was added to the insurance list. I told my accountant this was ludicrous and instructed him to tell the bureaucrat that we weren't going to hire anyone else. I also told him to ask the bureaucrat what would happen if a company closed, because I did not want to do business in Egypt if I had to deal with such mindless policy. Of course, I was bluffing.

My accountant did not solve the problem with that line of reasoning, but my name did. After fighting at length with the bureaucrat, Samer was asked the name of our company, the one with the resigned employee to be struck from the tax roll. No sooner did he mention our company's name than one of the bureaucrats who overheard him said, "That's Mr. Marshall who is the chairman?"

With the accountant's confirmation, my resigned employee was immediately struck from the tax roll. It was a simple bureaucratic task that my accountant had spent hours arguing. That a foreign manager was involved changed the matter. Was the bureaucrat looking for a bribe or following a stupid central government policy to prevent unemployment from rising? My accountant said he had likely been doing the former.

In meetings with bureaucrats, I figured that announcing I lived in Cairo might get me better service. At least the bureaucrat would know I could easily return if an error was made, a not-uncommon occurrence. With taxi drivers, declaring my residence in Cairo gave me some confidence that they would take the most direct route, knowing I was familiar with the streets. Egyptian taxi drivers fancy themselves political experts and responded to my admission of being American with "America is beautiful. Obama good." However, knowing that Gallup polls reported a loathing of America among Egyptians, I frequently responded, "America is good, but the government is bad." I did not truly feel that way—in fact, I feel very strongly about the virtues of the American system of government— but I wanted to defuse any hostilities.

Instances of international drama, such as an Egyptian criminal case against American nongovernmental organization (NGO) workers, meant I needed to be sensitive. With taxi drivers, I would pretend to be from Canada or Germany—more often the latter, since I spoke German and am a white Anglo-Saxon Protestant. Other times, I would ask the taxi driver to guess my nationality. Since our conversations were always in Arabic, I was frequently presumed to be French, Italian, or Lebanese. Never did they suggest the possibility that I could be American.

A year later, I wrote a check to the same government office to pay obligatory payroll taxes. I was surprised when a representative from the government showed up at our office to report that the check had bounced. I envisioned it had been piled on a desk for months, along with the mountain of loose papers I had seen. We had closed that bank account, and, sure enough, some bureaucrat had waited months to cash it. The government representative explained it had not been cashed because "it wasn't a lot of money." *Really?* I thought. The amount was several times the official monthly salary of a typical government employee, though maybe that bureaucrat's monthly *baksheesh* amounted to much more.

The author's office manager, Suzy Kamel, along with the author and his accountants, Talaat Ibrahim Hanna and Samer Talaat Hanna

The *baksheesh* is sometimes shockingly transparent, as though it were a performance fee. In another case, it was a referral fee. In Egypt, there is plenty of bureaucratic work one must delegate to his lawyer or agent. I wanted to authorize my lawyer to represent one of our firms in litigation matters, necessitating I sign a power of attorney. Such documents had to be in written Arabic, and I learned at the notary office that I had to be able to explain in Arabic what I was signing. My Arabic was fine for ordering food, but at that point it wasn't yet sufficient to understand Arabic legalese. That major milestone would come eighteen months later, when I explained in Arabic to an Egyptian bureaucrat that I was seeking to authorize my accountant to file forms on my behalf to start a new company. This time, however, I could not explain power of attorney over litigation matters. The notary informed me that I would need to call a certified translator, specifically the one for whom he had several business cards. Two hours later, Ismail the translator showed up and explained the document to me in barely comprehensible English. The translator's fee was EGP 150, about twenty-five dollars, and no sooner had I paid Ismail than he took a third of my fee, folding the EGP 50 bill in a small rectangle and slipping it into the desk of the government notary official . . . along with another of his business cards. Though de minimis in its amount, tea money became de rigueur when dealing with low-level bureaucrats. One had to carry a pocket full of EGP 5 notes everywhere.

When I overhear two people speaking a language I do not understand, I cannot help but feel that they are talking about me. I suspect this is not an uncommon paranoia. Having learned enough Arabic, I know the paranoia is largely imagined—well, mostly.

In yet another instance where I needed to explain to an Egyptian notary that I understood the document I was signing, I had kept mute. Samer was again with me, and I was there only to sign the form, preferring he handle the interaction with the notary while I caught up on some reading. That was when I heard it: The notary was talking specifically about me in Arabic, and I could not believe what I was hearing.

The bearded bureaucrat, obviously a religious conservative, announced to my accountant that he would not notarize anything for a foreigner. The notary had used a moderately derogatory word for foreigners, *khawaga*. I, standing next to my accountant, interjected in Arabic, "Who are you calling a foreigner? I speak Arabic. What do you want?"

My expectations of how life and business were to be conducted in Egypt usually proved incorrect and sometimes perfectly opposite of how reality usually unfolded. In this instance, though, the bureaucrat had erred in his expectation that a foreign could not speak Arabic. His assumption was to be expected, as not many expatriates did.

The bureaucrat tried to cover up his prejudice by asking if I knew what my accountant had brought me to the notary office for. I properly explained in Arabic the purpose of a power of attorney to him, to no avail. The bureaucrat searched through our corporate documents, claiming our governance document did not specifically endow me by name with signing authority for powers of attorney. What he would not acknowledge was Egyptian law vested that power to anyone who held the position of chairman of an Egyptian company. I was Chairman. The notary's frivolous reasoning proved useful enough for him to stubbornly refuse our request. On the way back from the office, I tried to find a reason for his behavior, something to explain his obvious hostility. The simplest explanation was probably the most likely: We should have paid him tea money.

6 DON'T STAND UNDER A TREE WHEN IT RAINS

Egypt's economy is heavily regulated. According to the Ease of Doing Business rankings published by the World Bank, starting a business in Egypt is remarkably simple, with Egypt measured as being among the easiest countries in which to incorporate. However, once business is underway, the difficulties mount: Complying with tax policy in Egypt is only slightly easier than doing so under the tax regime of India's infamous License Raj. It is more difficult to enforce contracts in Egypt than in the war-ravaged country of Iraq, and the legal system is approximately equal to that of Sudan. Yet business carries on. There is a market for everything in Egypt, and that market is mostly informal. The World Bank has reported that more than one of every three economic transactions in Egypt happens in the informal market, where participants ignore taxes and regulations on goods and services.

I became most educated in the black market for renting apartments, discovering that in addition to the difficulties posed by fifty-nine-year leases, I would also have to contend with illegal use changes and pre-dated contracts, which landlords had intentionally subjected to the onerous pre-1996 rent-control legislation. The thought seems nonsensical—after decades of earning below-market rent, why would a landlord sign a pre-dated contract, making it subject to rent control, when he could as easily sign a short-term free-market contract that offered much higher monthly rental income? The answer lay in money and psychology. I found that most building owners had not purchased buildings, as they, along with several relatives, had usually inherited them. Their proportional shares of rental income were modest, and they paid no costs in the property. Earning income through a rental building was like receiving part of an inheritance. When there was an opportunity to receive money, building owners chose the transaction that would result in the largest immediate payment. They would effectively sell the apartment according to the terms of a fifty-nine-year lease that had been pre-dated and would be subject to rent control. The result was a black market for "selling" apartments, as, though the law prohibited pre-dating contracts, the market did not.

The black market also disregarded zoning bylaws. Our lawyers determined that in Downtown, there had been a moratorium on zoning changes for as long as any bureaucrat could remember. Above-ground floors were mostly built for residential purposes, but in practice, the centrality of Downtown and the prevalence of government offices meant many such apartments were being used as offices. The practice was pervasive and ironic, as many of the unauthorized offices were law firms.

Black-market participants could not rely on the police or courts to resolve disagreements. One could not file a lawsuit to resolve a contract which was itself illegal. Instead, participants operated on the notion that possession was nine tenths of the law. Hence, in the rental market, black-market transactions were characterized by large initial payments through which the landlord would receive almost all of his compensation when the tenant took possession of the apartment. Fortunately for investors, there were options for dealing with the inefficiency of the Egyptian courts, such as the Cairo Regional Centre for International Commercial Arbitration. I always recommended specifying arbitration as the dispute resolution method when signing contracts in Egypt.

Other seemingly strange behavior mitigated the otherwise low-ranking performance of Egypt's court system. For example, with formal free-market rent contracts, landlords would seek to evict tenants as soon as they moved in. The same day the rent contract was signed, landlords would go to court, where they would ask for an eviction judgment to be post-dated to the end of the contract. Since legal proceedings were slow, landlords could not wait for tenants to overstay their contracts before beginning an eviction case. With an eviction ruling made months or years earlier but dated for the end of the contract, landlords could evict on the very day a tenant overstayed his or her contract. The development of this eviction technique made sense, given the glacial pace of Egyptian courts. It was also a waste of time and legal resources, as landlords jammed the courts despite the fact that most free-market tenants left amicably.

Egyptian courts were always overwhelmed, as third-party claimants would often file lawsuits to address injustices where none actually existed. Such was frequent as a plaintiff need not have legal standing. In many instances, no one had been harmed, or the aggrieved party had settled his or her claim outside the court, yet an activist—usually one of the many lawyers in which Egypt is awash—still filed a claim. This led to a flood of meaningless and ludicrous claims that clogged Egypt's court system. Even Napoleon Bonaparte was sued in the year 2013 for damage his troops had done to the Sphinx in 1798, and the plaintiff demanded an apology from the French people. The swift adjudication of business disputes would have been an incentive for participating in the formal economy, but in Egypt, the congested court system ensured that the informal economy would continue to thrive.

Outside my dealings with our planned real estate investment, I lived partly in the black market. Sure, the companies I chaired on behalf of my investors were part of the formal economy, and they were independently audited and were compliant with Egypt's multitude of tax laws, yet my life outside the office was overwhelmingly reliant on the informal economy, where there was a market for everything.

In Cairo, which had a growing population nearly twenty million strong, rising per-capita income, and heavily subsidized gasoline, the number of cars had grown rapidly in recent years. Traffic was notoriously burdensome, and parking was difficult, as evidenced by double parking on side streets. On busier streets, parking attendants claimed empty public parking spots by standing in them or placing a heavy object in the space. For those with means, the attendant would rent the spot for five or ten Egyptian pounds, about one or two American dollars, until the driver claimed his or her car. In front of my building, the attendants wore orange jackets and were all handicapped. One's limp left side suggested a previous stroke, another dragged an underdeveloped foot, and a third had a misshapen jaw that affected his speech. They were there every night, working, rendering a service with dedication I felt far exceeded that seen in the hard-luck cases of the West.

Parking attendants also ably facilitated double parking, acting as valets and shuffling cars around to allow drivers access to those parked nearest the curb. However, drivers who double parked often forewent the services of a valet, choosing to leave their cars in neutral, doors locked and unsupervised, allowing bystanders to push the car out of the way if the driver of a blocked-in car returned.

The black market helped with the difficulty of finding a parking spot. Though the government could have helped, too, it did not. Throughout Cairo, aged cars were abandoned in public parking spaces. Resting on deflated tires, the cars were always blanketed in a thick layer of dust. What would have served in the West as a perfect blank canvass for humorous finger writing, like "Wash me," rarely attracted such harmless graffiti—nor did it attract the attention of the government. One vehicle I saw daily was an older Russian Lada parallel parked across several "pull-in" spaces just outside the posh Gezira Sporting Club. A headlight was broken, the tires deflated, the license plate outdated. "Youssef" had scrawled his name across the windshield. I took a picture to serve as a reminder of how ineffectively the Egyptian government dealt with quality of life issues. A week later, something absurd happened: The adjacent roadway and parking spaces were repaved, but rather than removing the Lada, city workers paved around it, and the wheels of the car were asphalted in place.

The same dust and pollution that covered abandoned cars shortened the life of one's wardrobe, but it was rain that compounded the damage. The light khaki suit I frequently wore reflected the sun's intense heat, though it also showed evidence of any dirt. On a rare day when it rained in Cairo, I was caught outdoors, so I rushed to stand in the shelter of a thickly leaved tree. As the rain subsided, I noticed motorcycle drivers were having trouble remaining balanced. They had no better chance at remaining upright than a fawn attempting to walk across a frozen lake. Every time the motorcyclists braked at the intersection before me, they lost control. The wheels slid on leaked oil, which had coated the roadway. I was also coated, as the rain drops running off of the tree had cleansed months' worth of dirt and pollution that had been collected by each leaf. The entirety of my outfit looked as though a flock of seagulls had simultaneously targeted me. Thenceforth, I never stood under a tree when it rained in Cairo.

In Cairo, one could buy just about anything and have it delivered, save maybe for an umbrella. There was even a cell-phone application to order McDonald's delivery. A "Fespa"—there is no v in Arabic— was the most common delivery vehicle. Motorcyclists were required to don helmets, and deliverymen obliged, wearing helmets several sizes too large, which rattled and bounced about their heads. Civilians were more creative, if they wore helmets at all. Construction hardhats with a twine chin strap were used with some frequency.

I had gathered that trust was a rare commodity in Egypt, as I assumed the slothful court system would create opportunity for fraud, though I had not been subjected to such in day-to-day life.

Although I had been ripped off for silly items a few times, this never happened when I spoke Arabic to the vendor. The greatest test of trust came when I visited the US Consulate to renew my passport, its pages nearly full. Little did I know that I could not take electronic items into the consulate. The security guard pointed to a travel agency across the street, saying they would store my laptop. After handing over my computer, I returned to the consulate, where I realized I had not agreed to a storage fee. I worried my laptop would be held hostage for an exorbitant price, one I would pay if necessary.

Abandoned cars were a nuisance the Egyptian government ignored.

Services were often rendered without both parties agreeing to a price. Payment was made afterwards, the amount chosen by the buyer. Shoe shines were conducted this way, as were taxi rides and, apparently, laptop storage. When I finished at the consulate, I decided to give EGP 20, just over three dollars, to the attendant who had held my laptop. He voiced no objection, and I figured I had overpaid.

Not everyone was this trustworthy, or so I intuited. In Egypt, the poor often sell boxes of tissues to drivers stopped at intersections. When my taxi driver stopped to buy a box of tissues, I noticed that he shook the box near his ear as we drove off. I soon realized he was checking to see if there were tissues inside.

When there wasn't a market to be found, mass communication technologies helped. Several times, I received BlackBerry Messenger texts like this one:

*Urgent: a girl is dying now, she has blood cancer & needs blood type B+ urgent at ma3had naser Call amal 0100******4, if u can't donate pls fwd ,mayb u r the reason 4 her to live.*

And in the few instances where the market failed, people would pretend otherwise. A waiter once told me, without pausing, "Would you like white or brown bread? But today we have no brown bread."

7 ARABIC LESSONS

For tourists, Egypt is an English-language experience, as four- and five-star hotels and Nile cruises are uniformly staffed by English speakers. I, however, had employees and real estate brokers who did not speak a word of English. Pantomiming might have worked at the tourists' bazaar, but not in business. So I resolved to learn Arabic, attending classes three times a week in sessions each lasting two hours. My effort to speak Arabic provided no shortage of hilarity.

I was determined to practice my Arabic in everyday situations. Of course, I often made mistakes and usually only realized them much later. For a week, I had been addressing women with the male version of "please." Other times, my misspoken Arabic was immediately obvious and occasionally awkwardly so. Once, I thought I had told my office manager "Look," using the imperative, when I had actually said "Kiss me." After making me repeat myself and the mistake, she could no longer control her laughter.

There were other pairs of words whose Arabic pronunciations sounded quite similar. They too led to awkward situations when my modest ability to pronounce Arabic confused pyramid with crime, fruit with change from a bill, a man with a leg, an alphabetic character with sheep, a dog with a heart, and a building with a donkey.

Sometimes I would be too embarrassed to admit the mistake, like once at McDonald's. I thought I had said, "I want the quarter-pounder value meal, meal number three," and I had pointed to the overhead menu. What arrived was in triplicate: three quarter-pounders, three large fries, and three Cokes. As one does after having clumsily tripped on flat ground, I looked about to see if anyone was watching. Hoping no one was looking, I told the McDonald's server that I had changed my mind and to please put the food in a bag "to go." While walking with the food to my apartment, and when no one was looking, I threw away the two unwieldy sodas that I had mistakenly purchased.

I also made unspoken mistakes, cultural ones, like wearing a seat belt when taking a taxi in Egypt. Male passengers are expected to ride in the front seat of a taxi, women in the back seat, and the comfort afforded by the additional leg room was a welcome improvement over the cramped rear seats of Manhattan taxis. Sitting in the front seat also meant that most taxi rides would include conversations, though nonverbal actions would also illicit comments by the driver.

During my early days in Cairo, I reflexively reached for the seatbelt only to be told by the driver that I wouldn't need it, as he emphatically explained that he was a safe driver. This meant that my attempts to wear a seatbelt would be taken as an affront by most taxi drivers. However, wearing a seatbelt also had other consequences: Because taxi seatbelts are so rarely used, the accumulation of dirt on the belt leaves a sash-like mark across one's clothing. So, to reduce my cleaning bill, I rarely wore a seatbelt. The several car accidents I was in were unremarkable, as Cairo's habitual traffic jams limited the pace of cars to little more than ten miles per hour and meant accidents in town were rarely serious.

I was learning to speak Arabic, but my wife and parents advised me to begin looking Arabic, too. They suggested I should not "stick out as a foreigner." I promised I would be careful to not wear a baseball hat in public or walk around in sneakers, and I abided by that, save for whenever I walked to the sports club in my neighborhood. But that was my beat—all along the route, I knew the neighborhood fixtures, like the shoe-shine man, the newspaper vendor, and the proprietor of a junk-food stand. I felt comfortable greeting them in colloquial Arabic, sometimes stopping to discuss the news of the day.

However, speaking Arabic to the immigration officer thumbing through my American passport made me "stick out" as an Egyptian, something I had not intended nor thought myself capable of. That morning, I was departing for Europe, where I would switch to a Boston-bound flight. I handed my passport, ticket, and exit card to the Egyptian immigration official. She was a young woman in an unadorned police officer's uniform, and she looked more like a secretarial assistant than one of the state officials who manned the desks and checked travel documents. She wore a single ear piece which connected to her cellphone and likely filled the silence with Egyptian pop music.

That morning, in addition to a valid Egyptian residency visa, my passport was full of numerous visas to various countries, a half-dozen used Egyptian tourist visas, and an expired residency visa. I had been entering Egypt on tourist visas until I could obtain my residency visa, and this flustered the immigration official, as she was unable to find the currently valid visa. I had mistakenly forgotten to identify the valid visa, as I usually did when handing over my papers, so I blurted out in Arabic as she flipped past a page, "My visa is there. Sorry."

She looked up with an exceedingly stern face that I had not figured an unmarried twenty-something female officer could muster. She asked, "Where are your parents from?" At first, I could not understand her, as she hadn't spoken through the small hole in the glass that separated us. I asked her politely to repeat herself. She did: "Where are your parents from? Your father, is he Egyptian?" That was when I knew I had made a mistake. She was attempting to finger me as an Egyptian national traveling without having declared my nationality. Or, worse, she would ask me why I knew how to speak Arabic—xenophobia had been rising throughout my tenure in Egypt.

I responded that my father had a German name, and I enunciated it, "Stocker," before explaining that my mother was American. I had not lied, but I had not been precisely accurate, either. My father was American, his ancestors German. The official got to the heart of the matter, asking, "Are you Egyptian?"

"No," I answered. "I am American."

She stamped and returned my passport, and I resolved not to speak Arabic to Egyptian immigration officials again. Though I took that morning's exchange as a measure of my accent, I was just as worried that my competency would label me as part of the "foreign hand." During and following the uprising, the term referred to those who had supposedly sought to destabilize the Egyptian government and society.

I did not watch my first two-hour-long Egyptian movie until I had studied Arabic for two and a half years, and I took eight hours to watch the movie, frequently pausing the dialog to ask my tutor about vocabulary and culture. The movie, *Black Honey*, narrates the experiences of an Egyptian-American when he returns to current-day Egypt after having lived in the United States for twenty years. He finds Egypt poorer than he remembered it, and his extended family is down on their luck due to a dearth of jobs. In a melodramatic scene, he complains to his uncle about the indifference of Egyptians towards the difficulties of life in Egypt. The uncle responds by explaining the concept of *Elhamdulillah* (praise be to God).

Black Honey was one of the reasons I refuted an argument sometimes made by my friends in America. Whenever I made note of a less desirable condition in Cairo, like the pollution, friends would say, "The Egyptians probably don't mind. They don't have experience with anything better." I disagreed—Egyptians did know better. My regular taxi driver asked that I bring him a tire inflator from America, knowing there was better to be had outside of Egypt. He was right.

I feel most everyone who lives in underdeveloped countries knows that living conditions are better in other parts of the world. That others have it better does not worry Egyptians much, praise be to God. Egyptians also know, as explained in Black Honey, that life is much worse in some other places. For one, Egypt shares a border with Sudan, a country much worse off. Knowing this, I felt Egyptians were thankful to God that their fate was not worse. This concept of life, *Elhamdulillah*, may have also explained a word that was used with particular frequency: *malesh*. The best way I could ever translate this term was as "Shit happens," and given how often I heard *malesh* uttered, shit happened a lot in Egypt. Yet, knowing that life was better in other countries, Egyptians would soon demand better rather than accepting their current condition.

8 A WORLD IN A CITY

No sooner had I arrived to start our project in Cairo than an Egyptian real estate broker announced that I should not "surface." We figured the broker knew the best tactics to navigate the Egyptian market, and we agreed with his assertion that the sight of an American investor would inflate the asking prices of the assets we were trying to buy. So I hid, spending the first three months exclusively in the office, at the gym, or at Arabic lessons. Hiding meant I had not yet developed any friendships in Egypt and was made easier by the fact that our office was a large residential apartment. We had arranged the rooms to serve as office space but for a separate bedroom and bathroom that I called home for nearly three years. I soon grew restless, so I reached for my "passport to the world," as Winston Churchill defined it: my polo handicap.

Twenty years earlier, I had attended boarding school at Culver Military Academy. There I had played polo and was named the most valuable player during my last year. I continued to play polo at Cornell University but had played only once or twice a year since graduating. I was hardly in playing shape, but I connected with Egypt's polo federation president, Farouk Younes. He was a delightful and worldly Egyptian who spoke at least four languages and whom I rarely saw without his horsehair flyswatter, ivory cotton safari shirt, and jodhpurs. He had reached a five-goal handicap many decades earlier, that exemplary rating still virtually unheard of for an amateur player like Farouk when lesser-ranked players were good enough to make polo a career. Polo for Farouk was a lifestyle, never a career; the gentlemanly competition and social gathering were the draw for him, and so he ensured that the polo scene would have the same draw for us.

I attended a match between the Gezira Sporting Club's team and the team of Egypt's National Police Force. There I coincidentally reconnected with a boarding school friend, Mohamed El Sewedy, who had also played polo at Culver. After having been in Egypt for several months, I was delighted to see his familiar face. Mohamed and I had not spoken for the past twenty years, since he had graduated from Culver a year before I did. I remembered Mohamed as a quiet cadet during the first year we both shared at the academy, a fact he later explained was due to his rudimentary grasp of English. By the time he graduated Culver he had perfected his language skills and soaked up the institution's leadership training. Both were crucial to his role as a leading executive in his family's international manufacturing company. They exported power cables and electrical equipment to the region and Europe, which earned him the nickname "Switch," as in a light switch. The moniker was apropos, as Switch was always "on" whenever I saw him. Whether it was in business or sport, he was never idling. Though he too had stopped playing polo for a period, he now practiced with a zeal that I would never see rivaled during my tenure in Egypt. When he encouraged me to begin spending my weekends atop a polo pony, I jumped at the chance.

Months later, I was fit enough to join John Harris and Mohamed on the Gezira Sporting Club to defeat the Egyptian Police team in an intense match. I left the game with a knee injury only to have Mohamed try to rally my spirits, saying, "Just go sit in the middle of the field so we can beat the police!" Had we used a substitute player, our team's handicap would have increased, and our lead would have been erased. I would have trouble walking for several weeks until a compression bruise healed, but we won. After the match, I learned the police would go unpaid because of the game's result. This explained the very competitive nature of our opponent: They were semi-professionals who earned bonuses for victories. I still find it strange to think that in a country where forty percent of the population lives below the poverty line, the government would pay the police force's polo players for victories.

The polo connection also introduced me to John Harris, who would become my best friend in Cairo, and his wife, Nora, who would be a board member of my Egyptian companies. Yet I was surprised to find a third Culver Military Academy alumnus on the polo field. Karl Hilberg was stationed in Cairo as a commander with the US Navy and was active in the polo scene. Ten years my senior, Karl explained that Cairo would be his last overseas posting before he returned to serve one last tour in America before retiring. When I learned Karl had requested and been granted a rare waiver to extend his tour in Cairo, I began learning that some expatriates become enamored with the colonial lifestyle that Cairo offers. Naturally, Karl, Mohamed and I, along with John Harris, became a team and regularly defeated our opponents. Shortly after Karl's departure, John, Mohamed and I even won the first annual Egypt Cup, a national tournament held in Alexandria.

Polo would not be my only passport to the world. So too was the large number of embassies in Cairo. I have often been told that Cairo has more embassies than any other city in the world. Even North Korea maintained an embassy in Cairo, and the US Embassy's diplomatic mission there was our nation's largest permanent embassy in the world. This meant that when I stopped for coffee anywhere in my neighborhood, I would sometimes bump into other expatriates usually affiliated with their home governments, like Robert Becker, who was the only American to remain in Egypt to stand trial on charges of conducting political work on behalf of an illegal non-governmental organization.

Nora, John and I were dining with several other friends when

Robert arrived in the middle of the meal. Nora had invited him so we could hear firsthand about his tribulations. He looked and sounded to me like a tough democratic operative, a James Carville type. Becker had been working with the National Democratic Institute (NDI) to teach campaign principles to anyone, including Islamists, who wanted guidance on conducting political outreach. For this effort, Robert had just been interrogated by Egyptian officials, and he wondered whether he would be charged along with his superiors. Later, he found out that he would be.

Besides regularly bumping into Robert at a particular Costa Coffee café in my neighborhood within Zamalek, I would occasionally start conversations with strangers there. One morning, an Arab-looking male sat next to me, reading an Arabic newspaper. His attire consisted of a sport coat and dressy pants. Both were rather formal for the weekend. He passed a glossy one-page advertisement to me, as his paper had come with two copies of the same ads. He said something in French, a language for which I only had maybe twenty-five hours of formal training. After replying to him in French that I did not speak the language, he switched to Arabic.

I did not recognize his Arabic accent and couldn't fully understand him. After he repeated himself, I realized he was commenting on the remarkable amount of food in the family meal advertised by a local fast food chain. I agreed it was a good deal but jokingly added, "Only if you're hungry! I could never eat that much alone." We then continued in a third language, English, talking about trivialities. I learned he was an Algerian Embassy official. Though he looked to be the age of a grandfather, he produced from his wallet a very dated picture of his wife and young children. The faded photo had to have been at least fifteen years old. Later, I would wonder why he didn't have a newer one.

I asked if he was the Algerian ambassador. He said no and that he had previously been stationed in Vienna, Austria. Vienna being one of my favorite cities, we agreed it was a beautiful place. He replied that he spoke German, too, yet we only exchanged a few words. He must not have known the language well, or perhaps he had last spoken German when his family photo was taken, quite some time ago. We wished each other a nice day as he departed.

The diversity of Cairo's population meant that restaurants specializing in regional cuisine were not hard to come by. Restaurants offering more adventurous cuisines relied on the strength of their cooking rather than an inviting atmosphere or memorable name. The succinctly named "Yemeni Restaurant" was evidence of this, as, though lacking any creativity in its name, the restaurant offered better fare than I had enjoyed in Sana'a. At the comparably named "Sudanese Restaurant," expense was spared on dishes and cutlery, as guests were offered neither. Napkins were a roll of paper towels, and drinking water was self-service from a single cooler. A communal cup was provided and, as I recall, chained to the water cooler. We opted for bottled water and the waiter's recommended fare. Using crepe-like bread to scoop from a communal dish, we sampled the delicious meat and sauce. The flavor was unique and tasty. The meat, though? I stopped asking what kind of meat I was eating when I learned that my favorite Egyptian street sandwich, a shawarma, was made of camel meat. Meals were inevitably inexpensive at these dives, which doubled as culinary gems. A full dinner, water included, had cost us about $4.50 each.

At the Sudanese restaurant, John noted that portraits of both Northern Sudanese President Omar Al-Bashir and southern freedom fighter John Garang were hung above the door. The waiter explained to him that conflict was best left to politicians: In his restaurant, everyone was welcome.

That my dining experiences in Cairo were particularly colorful was partly by necessity. I was not a US government employee with access to the commissary and its American products. There, after passing through security rivaling that of the US Embassy, American civil servants could buy Oscar Mayer bacon, duty-free Budweiser beer, and even American ice at Walmart-like prices. Those perks, I assumed, supplemented their modest government salaries, until I learned the average salary for a US federal employee was twice that paid in the US private sector. The cost of delivering American-made ice to the North African desert of Cairo where it was on sale in the commissary must have been a princely sum. Whatever the cost, I would have paid it to avoid "Ramses' revenge," as my American partner called it. On each of my first four trips to Cairo, I succumbed to the intestinal disturbance. When I finally moved to Cairo, I began brushing my teeth in tap water and never suffered the affliction again. I also began eating the slices of raw onion which were habitually served with Egyptian meals. The same sulfur compounds in the vegetable which cause people to cry purportedly contain antimicrobial elements that fight E. coli and salmonella bacteria.

Camels on the way to market

Just as Cairo was a United Nations of restaurants, so too was it home to some of our adversaries' embassies. The Iranian embassy was in a nearby but low-rent district, while the Chinese and North Korean embassies were both in my neighborhood and only blocks away from my apartment. Both had glass-enclosed display cases mounted to their exterior walls for pedestrians to view. The photos displayed their armed forces conducting military exercises, and the North Korean Embassy specifically showed the late Kim Jong-Il leading every military activity.

Improving my understanding of geopolitical news and the way in which international developments were perceived by other nations was a valuable experience. Trying to adopt another's perspective helped. For example, I thought about the Egyptian view that foreign NGO workers should have been jailed for teaching political campaign tactics. How would I feel if another country did the same in America? How would America feel if the Chinese or Saudi Arabian governments funded charitable organizations in the US, especially organizations that taught Americans how to more effectively participate in politics? The exercise radically simplified the issue for me: I would be shocked to find another country operating inside the US political process the way we had in Egypt. The underlying meaning was too strong, as it could seem that America was influencing the activities of Egyptian politicians and their parties. After a seventeen-month trial, the Egyptian judiciary had a similar reaction and sentenced Robert Becker to two years in jail with hard labor. The facts of the case I knew suggested Robert should have been declared not guilty. Those, though, conflicted with the prevailing political sentiment, a sentiment I could now appreciate. Robert exiled himself from Egypt hours after the verdict.

Using this reversal-of-position tool, I wondered how pedestrians would have reacted to pictures depicting American military exercises. They would react negatively, of course. How could North Korea and China get away with such provocative pictures, attempting to assert their military power? Was it because neither had invaded foreign lands of late? Would those two nations have displayed such pictures outside their Washington embassies? North Korea definitely would not—they had no embassy in Washington.

9 RELIGION: YOU'D BETTER GET ONE

Blasphemy is a criminal offense in Egypt. During my time in Cairo, at least one high-profile atheist was sentenced to jail for contempt of religion. On my application for a residency visa, I was required to declare my religion, and my choices were few: Jew, Christian, or Muslim. There were no other recognized faiths, nor was I allowed to declare myself an atheist. These were but a few of the signs that in Egypt, religion was interwoven with government. I not only learned about Islam but also found that Coptic Christianity, a form of Christianity which dates to the fourth century, was a completely foreign belief system to me.

The Muslim call to prayer cannot be escaped. The prayer schedule is lunar, with the earliest of the five daily chants beginning around three thirty in the morning. Even at that early and silent hour, imams project their prayer verses through amplified speakers outside each mosque. Though Muslims should heed the call to prayer, most do not, choosing instead to pray at more convenient times. Sublimation toward Mecca was most often performed in private, with prayers being a rote set of upright and kneeled movements that lasted about seven minutes. Only infrequently did I see a man pray in a public space. These public prayers were usually performed by police officers or guards who could not leave their posts or by manual laborers who worked outdoors. More common was to find small stores temporarily closed while clerks prayed.

I found myself nearly interrupting a Muslim's prayer several times, most notably at my favorite shawarma stand, where I had befriended the cook. The shawarma is the Middle Eastern version of fast food: spit-roasted meat prepared with a heavy dose of animal fat. Tahini, a sesame seed sauce I loved, spicy sauce, and pickles were the usual condiments, along with parsley, onions, and tomatoes.

Chef Mohamed was conservative. He donned a full beard, four years in length, and with no moustache. I understood this to have been the grooming habit of the Prophet Mohamed. He smiled often but kept his mouth closed to shield his rotted and missing teeth. They reflected years of smoking cigarettes and drinking heavily sweetened tea, both common vices in Egypt. We exchanged greetings whenever I passed the spit that he tended most evenings. I was surprised to see, more than a year after the uprising, when men were increasingly donning lengthy beards, that Mohamed had shortened his to a length not much longer than my month's worth of facial hair. I had asked him the reason, and he replied vaguely about it having become too long. I suspected the truth was that he did not want to be associated with the organized conservative Muslim *salafi* sect, which was becoming an increasingly vocal and divisive group in Egypt. His shawarma spit was in the heart of Egypt's most liberal neighborhood, Zamalek. His beard may have been jeopardizing his job. Though we mostly spoke of trivialities, like the weather or the street cat to which he would toss scraps, he also knew French and some English. As was expected with any service rendered to me in Egypt, I obligingly tipped him one pound ($0.17) per shawarma.

On one visit, I went to the cashier to pay for my shawarma. I immediately recognized the back of the young, hapless, slick-haired Egyptian who was the regular cashier. He was hunched behind the counter, and I figured he was picking up coins he had dropped. When his task wore on my patience, I opened my mouth, only to bite my tongue when I saw the corner of his prayer rug. Interrupting a Muslim's prayer sequence would have been extremely bad etiquette.

The prayer rituals of Coptic Christians, however, were not celestially timed, being instead related to the proximity of a church. I always relied on the punctuality and expected piety of Ramon, a Coptic taxi driver whom I often called. Whenever we passed a Coptic church, he would move his hand about his chest in the outline of a cross and whisper a prayer. The docents at three Coptic monasteries proved as reliable—I found it necessary to wait for my guides to touch or kiss certain relics and images before I asked about each nave we admired.

Shawarma Chef Mohamed

Muslims often add the phrase *Inshallah* ("God willing") immediately after a verbal commitment. Some Coptic Christians also utter the words. The religious phrase means that any future activity, such as a business meeting, will happen unless by reason of God's will. When arrivals to appointments are delayed by traffic, emails not returned due to an excess of work, or meetings cancelled to address more pressing matters, I assumed they believed God's will was at fault.

The "big beards," as some of my Muslim friends labeled the more conservative Muslims and with whom Chef Mohamed seemed not to be associated, usually also donned *zibibas*. This raisin-shaped mark is formed by the habitual motion of one's forehead hitting the prayer rug. Some *zibibas* were so calloused and bruised that I accepted the explanation that some Muslims placed a stone underneath their prayer rugs. In my travels throughout the Mideast, this *zibiba* was almost exclusive to Egyptian men. I was not the only one to suspect that these *zibibas* had been manufactured. Sultan Al Qassemi, a leading Arab commentator, tweeted a similar suspicion: "How do people who have been praying for 15 years on soft carpets & prayer mats have a Zabiba the size of Zimbabwe on their forehead?"

My office manager, Suzy Kamel, was Coptic Christian. She had the Coptic cross tattooed on the inside of her wrist, which seemed the location of choice for Coptic women. I noticed that lower-class Coptic men inked the cross on the prominent fold between the thumb and index finger. For Suzy, the religious marking had been indelibly inked at a very young age and without her consent. She explained that traditionally, Coptic children were baptized on the same day once a year, a Sunday before Easter. At the ceremony, parents often requested that a cross be tattooed on their child. Baptized and confirmed as a Lutheran, I had grown up being taught that the body is a temple and that one should not lay a mark upon it. Christianity in Egypt might have shared the same name as the religion into which I was baptized, but it sure was much different in practice.

I shared holidays, like Christmas, with the Copts, but in concept only. December 25 was a work day in Egypt, as Christmas came two weeks later on January 7, according to the Coptic calendar. Easter was also off schedule from that of Western Christians. Though something like half of all American marriages end in divorce, Coptic Christians had a different view of the matter. Divorce was prohibited under all circumstances, except in cases of adultery. This divorce prohibition was a frequent cause of Egypt's worst bouts of sectarian violence.

Coptic women who sought divorce sometimes converted to Islam, since Muslims were not prohibited from divorcing. As a Muslim, a formerly Coptic woman would be granted a divorce, but religious conversions in Egypt were a sensitive matter. Coptic women often attempted to immediately convert back to Christianity, the conversion to Islam having been a mere practicality. This was when troubles started: In a few instances, one side, Muslim or Christian, would accuse the other of kidnapping the forlorn bride. Shootings then erupted and churches were burned, including one in the impoverished neighborhood of Imbaba, where my butler lived, just across the Nile from Zamalek.

Religion sometimes interfered with business or complicated the personal freedoms to which I was accustomed. Most notable was Ramadan, a thirty-day religious observance that requires Muslims to fast during daylight hours. Fasting was another matter to Copts, but for Muslims it was strict: nothing, not even water. Some Muslims even avoided brushing their teeth for fear they might swallow water. At sunset during the month of Ramadan, large meals were served. I found it strange but reasonable that Egyptians consumed a disproportionate amount of food during the month of Ramadan and, on average, gained weight. They also had trouble getting any work completed during Ramadan. With evening dinners lasting well into morning hours and the most sensible activity to avoid hunger being sleeping, work hours were ten in the morning to three in the afternoon, at best. Little was accomplished during Ramadan, making the weeks that preceded the month-long observance harried. Personally, I used the month to return to America and catch up on administrative work there, but not before I was expected to pay bonuses to our staff.

A Coptic monk explaining his Christianity

I learned that bonuses were paid to Egyptian employees two or three times per year. Bonuses in Egypt are usually paid at the beginning of Ramadan, at the end of Ramadan, and two weeks later upon another Muslim holiday. These payments are a critical component of employee compensation, even for menial labor, and are expected.

The logic of consolidating bonuses into a six-week period made no sense to me. I dispensed with that policy when I took over our Egypt operations. Bonuses became a semi-annual affair: June and December. As I explained to our employees, they would also be based on performance. After I explained the policy of semi-annual bonuses to a junior staff lawyer, he still asked if he would be receiving a bonus at the next Ramadan. I proposed to withhold money from his salary and deliver that money at Ramadan, like a forced savings plan. He declined.

My life is richer for having lived in Egypt, where my white Anglo-Saxon Protestant background was not only a minority but also nearly absent from the population. Yet my sensitivities were sometimes tested by others' religious traditions. Such was the case during Eid al-Adha. My expatriate friends with young children all left town during this holiday, which came two months after the end of Ramadan. Eid al-Adha is celebrated by Muslims to commemorate the willingness of Abraham to sacrifice his son Ishmael as an act of obedience to God. God, having intervened, provided Abraham with a sheep to sacrifice instead. In Egypt, sheep, goats, or cows served that purpose. In the weeks leading up to the holiday, shepherds moved their flocks to the inner city. There the creatures were sold, bled, and slaughtered in public following the Eid prayer.

Just as an apple is shined, I saw shepherds tease the coats of their animals to give them a more portly appearance. For poorer consumers, this would be a major purchase that would feed their extended family. For the wealthier, Eid al-Adha would be an occasion for charity.

The first time I was in Cairo during Eid al-Adha, my Coptic Egyptian friends advised me to stay indoors. I ignored them. When I walked that day to my sporting club for a workout, a swim, and some sun, I noticed a young cow, cute and mooing, tied to a tree across the street from my flat. When I returned hours later, the cow hung from the tree over a large pool of blood, slaughtered. I found nothing offensive about the sight, as humans eat beef. However, the stench of blood was unpleasant. Worse, blood was on the streets throughout the city. Days later, my office staff and I had to fend off the flies that logically followed.

The following year, I observed the holiday's charitable component. Poor Egyptians, whose dress gave them away, had travelled to my borough, the richest in Cairo. From my prospect in a coffee shop, I observed them running about the block as if there were an Easter egg hunt underway. One would shout, and the others would scurry in his direction. A few minutes later, they would carry away plastic shopping bags full of raw meat given to them in charity. The whole scene would have been a lot to explain to a young child: Animals were slaughtered in plain sight, an underclass seeking handouts of raw meat, all despite the stench. My friends were wise to ferry their children out of Egypt for the holiday.

Animals were not the only corpses I saw during my time in Egypt. Local newspapers showed little restraint with images of traumatic injuries, often publishing photos of dissidents killed during times of political instability. The most gruesome were the bodies crushed under army vehicles. Those images flooded YouTube and Twitter, as the army was in control of the country at the time. There was a limit to the criticism the army would tolerate, yet it was the indifference of people stepping around a dead body that proved the harsh reality of life in a Third-World country: Governments were not efficient enough to shield us from the sight of death. I had been a volunteer firefighter and EMT for a number of years and knew the sight of a corpse, rigid and purplish. I saw that same evidence in a body that lay on the side of the road I took to get to polo practice. I did not announce the sight to my Egyptian friend who was driving us that morning.

For that matter, I rarely complained to my Egyptian friends. I even went so far as to block my Egyptian friends from viewing pictures I posted to my Facebook account under the album title "Not so great." There I had posted images of an industrial pail labeled as radioactive, which was being used to hold building waste. I also captured images of the polluted haze that smothered Cairo. I figured nothing could be gained by pointing out the shortcomings I found in my hosts' country. If I knew, surely my Egyptian friends knew, too. The government barely functioned when it came to addressing even the most obvious of issues, such as removing a pauper's corpse.

Not until I had been in Egypt for six months did I realize that the only siren I ever heard was that of the police tow truck. With owners of double-parked cars scurrying back at the sound of the siren, police officers saved themselves the trouble of getting out and immobilizing the double-parked car with a boot. How legally parked cars, blocked in by booted cars, ever left was a riddle I never solved. Having never seen a fire truck or any police action beyond issuing parking tickets, I bought a fire extinguisher for my apartment.

Some religious traditions confused me. The sale of "fasting desserts" highlighted one such case. A coffee shop poster advertised apple tart and cherry cake amongst sugary delights labeled as fasting desserts. I asked the wrong person, the coffee shop manager, what a fasting dessert was. He did not know. That his name was obviously Muslim—Ahmed, Mohamed, or Moustafa, I do not remember which—should have tipped me off: These were desserts advertised during Lent.

Coptic Christians fast during Lent, but they do not practice Muslim fasting, abstinence from consumption. No, the rules are a bit more complicated. When I asked my Coptic office manager how a list of desserts could possibly be allowable during a fast, she explained fasting meant not eating animal products. A cherry cake was devoid of animal products, and that made it a permissible indulgence even for the pious. The irony was not lost on me.

My sacrifice was pork. With ninety percent of the Egyptian population being Muslim, there was not a large demand for pork, except amongst the Coptic minority. Poorer Copts raised pigs, fattening them on discarded food scraps collected from the garbage.

When the swine flu became a global contagion, Egyptian officials oversaw the culling of all 300 thousand pigs in the country. Health officials overlooked that swine flu was a moniker only and completely unrelated to pigs. As well, no one in Egypt had caught the swine flu, but with pig farmers uncompensated for the loss of their herds, pork disappeared from the marketplace.

One need not abstain from eating desserts when fasting

Where there is a demand, a market will arise, and in Egypt there is a market for everything. Maadi, a Cairo suburb with a high concentration of expatriates, soon had a German meat market that sold flown-in frozen pork. While the slaughtering of pigs had been outlawed in Egypt, selling imported finished meat products was not. A pound of bacon cost twelve dollars, double the market price in any developed country.

Then there was alcohol. Forbidden under Islam, tipple was a

delicate matter. When invited to social obligations at a Muslim household, it was best to leave the bottle of wine at home. Flowers were better gifts. However, individual Muslims had varied tolerances for alcohol. Besides imbibing, some Muslims even worked as bartenders, though the profession was predominantly a Coptic one. There was a very high tax on imported alcohol, so one avoided consuming taxed alcohol if possible. One way around the tax was to bring your own liquor to the restaurant. I usually kept a bottle of whiskey at the restaurant Don Quichotte (pronounced *donkey shot* by Egyptians), where one was charged a twenty-five-dollar corkage fee once per bottle regardless how many visits it took to finish the poison.

The duty-free import of alcohol was allowed in limited amounts. With taxed liquor so outrageously expensive and hard to even find for sale, most expatriates smuggled liquor. I did. There were even modest bragging rights for personal smuggling records. A close friend claimed to have once brought sixteen bottles from Lebanon, quadruple his allowance. If one ran out of alcohol, one could find reasonably priced locally made wine at Drinkies, one of only a handful of liquor stores in the entirety of Cairo. Though there were vineyards in Egypt, Egyptian wine was of universally poor quality. Still, at six dollars per bottle, stores did a swift business in the ripple. Locally made spirits were also available at Drinkies, though they had a stigma to overcome. For years, bathtub liquor had been marketed under poorly disguised knockoffs of brand names, such as "Johanna Talker" whiskey and "Gorodon's" gin.

Little more than a year after the January 25 uprising, I was scrolling through Twitter messages. In one, a complaint was being lodged against a local watering hole I frequented. The bouncer had turned away a veiled woman. I am sure she was just wearing the *hijab*—a usually stylish scarf that covered a woman's hair, ears, and neck—instead of a full veil. In a flash, I realized I had never seen a veiled woman in that bar or any bar in Cairo. Two months later, I first witnessed a covered Muslim woman at Apperitivo. About that same time, I realized that Drinkies' name and phone number had been removed from their black and orange delivery scooters. The uprising in Egypt had brought Islamists into majority rule. Now Drinkies delivered incognito, and Muslims were going to bars for a juice rather than a stiff drink.

Apperitivo's food was adventurous. Oxtail, tongue, and brain reflected the breadth of the Egyptian palate. The décor included wood paneling, soft lighting, and a leather-padded ceiling, and the bar was stocked with imported liquor and tended by an Egyptian wearing a dinner jacket. After numerous attempts, I never found a proper martini on offer. I learned the difference between ordering a martini and a "martini cocktail" right away: If I omitted asking for a cocktail, I could expect a glass of Martini, the sweet Italian wine used to flavor the Western martini. That was the only time I have sent back a drink to be remade. So, because one cannot screw up whiskey and soda water, I became a whiskey drinker.

10 TAXIING CHANGE IN A COLONIAL CITY

Before becoming a partner in our Egypt project, I had worked as an investment manager in Boston. Commuting from the suburbs, I left my house every day at five in the morning for the thirty-minute drive to my downtown gym and office. I rarely returned home until seven or eight. It was an exhausting and unsustainable workweek of seventy hours of more. Weekends also included work, my ethic seemingly apropos to that of Boston's Puritans. Although our Egypt fund intended to have me in Cairo for half of my time, separated from my wife, she and I felt our quality of life would improve.

Egyptian consultants were to handle in-country operations on a full-time basis, and my time in Boston would be spent working from home, where I would see my wife more often. That I would later assume in-country leadership duties meant I would actually see much less of Boston and my wife than we had expected. During the three years of our fund's life, I spent three quarters of my time in Egypt, time without my wife. That was difficult, as she is my best friend.

Though living without my wife was challenging, our relationship survived. We had Skype and Apple's FaceTime to keep us connected and our marriage intact. Mitigating the marital strain, my quality of life improved in other ways I had not expected. For one, in Egypt, there was no expectation that work would be conducted on weekends. I had penned emails on the weekend only to discover my lawyers, accountants, and real estate brokers rarely responded until the workweek resumed.

In the hyper-competitive environment of investment banking and asset management, a forty-hour workweek was unheard of. I had certainly never had the "part-time" experience of a forty-hour week. Having a weekend in Egypt allowed me a life. I studied Arabic, played polo, dined with friends, and undertook writing this book. I began to wonder if I could ever go back to the grind of a financial career in America.

Cairo offered a colonial lifestyle, which meant the luxury of inexpensive help. There was always someone willing to complete every chore. My butler handled cooking, cleaning, and shopping responsibilities. Our building's porter carried my luggage. Friends had live-in nannies costing no more than $650 per month. Their full-time gardeners and drivers cost two thirds less. Bureaucratic chores, like renewing my visa, were handled by paralegals whose ostensible skill was standing in line and whose knowledge was in which line to stand.

However, the colonial lifestyle was sometimes awkward. At the private Garden City Club, waiters were Sudanese. The club's management had outfitted the wait staff in formal dress, but it was the waiters' exceptional deference to patrons that made me feel as though I were on a plantation. Knowing that some Sudanese immigrants were escaping atrocities in their homeland, I understood they were making a better life for themselves in Cairo, where they had jobs, earned money, and found a community.

For the adventurous, a plethora of experiences could also be had for cheap. In Cairo, I was introduced to the Uyghur cuisine. For a total of EGP 106 ($17.66), I and five friends enjoyed the food of

China's western Muslim population. We enjoyed numerous spicy dishes of food and all left satiated. Some of the Uyghurs were in Cairo to study at the world's most prestigious institution of Sunni Muslim education, El Azhar. Judging from the stacked boxes of Chinese-labeled imported goods outside the restaurant, the Uyghurs also plied Chinese goods on Egyptian consumers.

The author and his butler, Tarek Zakry

Just as my day-to-day life had changed from what I knew in Boston, Cairo itself was undergoing changes. On my first visit to Cairo, black and white taxis were ubiquitous. They were mostly old Russian Ladas, French Peugeots, or Italian Fiats with body panels painted in alternating colors. All had antiquated mechanical meters, which, without exception, were never used. Instead, the fare was always negotiated. Taxi drivers explained to me that the metered rate was not fair, insufficient to cover their costs. For local residents, there was little to negotiate. Fares were a multiple of the five-pound note ($0.83) and a function of distance and neighborhoods traversed. However, unlike in New York City or Boston, taxi drivers were not required to accept a passenger's destination. Flagging a taxi meant announcing your destination through the open passenger window. A quick nod or "Ah," slang for yes, from the taxi driver was necessary. Taxi drivers avoided destinations that might leave them stranded in gridlocked parts of town. Such was the case where I lived, in Zamalek. Schools emptied at about two thirty, clogging roads and making walking more efficient. For this reason, I occasionally had trouble finding a taxi willing to take me to Zamalek in the early afternoon. I suspected less trouble befell me than Egyptians. To taxi drivers, I looked like an easy mark, a Westerner who could be charged an above-market fare.

With the gradual introduction in 2008 of the white taxi, passengers were afforded a metered ride and air conditioning. These new taxis had electronic meters whose fares proved remarkably similar to those negotiated in an unmetered black taxi. The Egyptian government, recognizing Cairo's extremely polluted air, outlawed taxis that had been manufactured more than twenty years earlier. To compensate taxi drivers whose cars had been built when leaded fuel was in vogue, the government offered loan guarantees on the purchase of a new taxi. As well, a subsidized option most taxi drivers chose was to convert the vehicle to run on natural gas. This certainly improved air quality, and during shortages of imported gasoline that followed the 2011 uprising, natural gas was readily available. It was produced domestically and probably in excess supply, given that the natural gas pipeline to Israel was bombed more than a dozen times after the uprising, which led the Israelis to cancel their contract to purchase Egypt's natural gas.

Customers of white taxis expected the fares to be determined by a digital meter. Yet, while the colors of taxis had changed, the taxi drivers proved recalcitrant. Drivers quickly invented ways to inflate fares. Aided by their talkativeness as experts on most matters, taxi drivers sometimes pretended to overlook turning on the meter. My habit became to make sure the meter was running and started at the base fare, EGP 2.50 ($0.42). However, on several occasions I was remiss. In one instance, I was half asleep, headed to the airport at four in the morning.

The trip at that hour was without hindrance, the roads empty, and normally cost me EGP 35 ($5.83) on a legitimate meter. In cases where the driver neglected to start the meter, it was best not to mention the situation while en route, or else price negotiation would begin immediately. This never happened to my friends or me, but a driver could leave one short of his or her destination if the ideal fare was not extracted. Instead, it was best to wait until arrival and then pay the driver by handing over the money from outside the car. I inevitably wound up paying an extra five pounds whenever I forgot to check whether the meter was running. If I had not learned the proper fair from several previous trips, I am sure I would have ended up paying double the metered rate.

Sometimes, the meter was already running when I entered a taxi. Perhaps the previous fare had remained on the meter or the driver had been driving about, accruing what always seemed to be a modest five or ten pounds extra on the meter. That amount, in most instances, doubled one's fare. The most nefarious were drivers who manipulated their meters to run faster than the regulated EGP 1.25 ($0.21) per kilometer. This made knowledge of the correct fare critical. When I knew the meter was running too quickly, drivers accepted a fare that was half the metered rate. I just pointed out that the meter was malfunctioning to which the driver inevitably agreed.

Taxi drivers became less cooperative in Egypt's post-uprising security vacuum. I discovered this during an early morning phone call. At four in the morning during November 2012, I received a call from an American graduate student I had seen at several parties. We were merely acquaintances, and I figured the call had been an accident. I had done the same when stuffing my phone into my pocket, as keys and coins could press against the dial pad. I did not answer. Then he called again. This, I suspected, was not a mistake. I replied with a text message asking him what was happening, to which he responded by calling me a third time. The conversation could have come from a movie:

William: Marshall, can you hear me?

Me: Yeah, dude. I'm sleeping. What's up?

William: Marshall, I can't hear you. Are you there?

At this point, I could hear loud Arabic conversations in the background.

Me: Yeah, I'm here. What's up?

William: I'm having a legal problem. I need you to call the US Embassy. Give them my social security number. It's . . .

Me: Wait. Let me get a pen.

I sprang out of bed. William relayed his social security identification number once, quickly. I barely had time to write down his words.

Me: What's the problem? Where are you?

William: I can't talk right now. Just call the Embassy.

The phone clicked, and the line went silent. Wow, I thought. What was that? I hadn't been able to make out the Arabic conversations I heard in the background of his call, but I envisioned him seated in a police station somewhere, police officers debating how to handle whatever legal problem he had found himself in. I called the US Consulate, the office responsible for addressing the needs of Americans traveling or residing in a foreign country.

I reached an Egyptian speaking perfect but accented English. He was concerned William was playing a joke on me, particularly in the absence of any information besides my acquaintance's name and social security number. I confessed it was limited information, but I was doing as anyone who was called at four in the morning should, even for a distant relation. After a maddening negotiation with him, he passed me to the duty officer. I gave her William's cell phone number and conveyed his message, and she promised to look into the issue.

I tried ringing William the next morning. No answer. I called a mutual friend and asked if he had any information about William. He did: William had called him, a bit drunk, early in the morning, mentioning that he planned to attend a party at the Four Seasons hotel. I suspected William had probably been picked up for public intoxication, yet I had never heard of this happening to anyone. I imagined arresting a foreign national and dealing with the resultant intervention of a foreign government created headaches for which beat officers did not care. So when I received a text message later in the morning from our mutual friend, it shocked me: *Just talked to William, it read. He's fine. They accused him of being an Israeli spy.*

William had been involved in a disagreement over taxi fare, which had led to accusations that he was a Zionist spy. I made note to budget a little extra for taxi fares even though only a minority of taxi drivers attempted to rip me off.

The best taxi ride I ever had in Cairo was in a white taxi piloted by a driver whose beliefs, I suspected, made him a sworn enemy of my country and me. I flagged him down and noticed the passenger window was closed. Not able to holler my destination to him for approval, I hopped into the front seat. I saw his ankles first. He was wearing sandals and black socks, and his light tan galabeya, a dress-like traditional garment, reached only as far as his calves. I looked up from his feet only to be immediately distracted by the bushy black beard that covered much of his face, save for above his upper lip. The top of his head was covered with a *kufi*, a crocheted cap seemingly worn in some fashion by the devout in every Abrahamic religion. So too were beards, I later deduced. He was a Salafi, a rigidly conservative Islamist, and there was no mistaking the fact.

I greeted him a "Good afternoon." He responded with the identical greeting, adding, "May you be blessed by God." He spoke the formal Arabic used in the Quran and responded to my announced destination with *Inshallah*. His taxi was spotless and air conditioned. Both explained why he had not lowered his passenger window, as Cairene taxi drivers rarely used air conditioning, preferring to drive about with their windows down, which invited desert dust onto every surface in a car. We made small talk, and when we arrived at my destination, I fumbled for the combination of bills and coins to pay the fare when I notice he had already assembled several coins as change. This had never happened to me. Taxi drivers never volunteered to give me change: They expected to keep it as a tip.

I explained this experience to my Coptic Christian office manager, who was not surprised. She said the Salafi taxi driver likely truly believed God was watching him, judging him on his honesty. He would not cheat me on the fare or the change. She also said that he would have never stopped to give her a ride.

Most taxi drivers in Cairo were quite colorful, even if they were remarkably uninformed. They often told jokes and commented on politics. Just as the colors of their cars were changing from black to white, Cairo was also changing me. I was becoming desensitized to certain harsh realities of living in a Third-World country. Most importantly, I was learning life and business in Egypt was much different than what I had known in the West. Still, first encounters with those differences reminded me just how far I was from my American home.

At a building that housed a broker's office, bloody handprints lined the entrance hall, and I stopped in my tracks. Had this been a crime scene? No: Those were for good luck. I learned the handprints were evidence that an animal, likely a cow or sheep, had been slaughtered on site. The animal's meat had been distributed to the neighborhood's poor, an act of charity that was considered good luck by Muslims. The almost always amateur butcher left bloodied handprints to create some permanency of the event. From time to time I would see those handprints near the entrances of buildings, usually in poorer neighborhoods. I even noticed that the adjoining groom's quarters at a friend's stables were bedecked by well-shaped, carefully placed blood-inked handprints.

A sight to which I became even more accustomed was veiled women. With nine out of ten Egyptians being Muslim, an only slightly smaller percentage of Egyptian women wore some sort of head covering. Long sleeves were de rigueur for women, as were covered legs. The few Muslim women who were uncovered were most always members of the very highest socioeconomic class. Some covered women wore the hijab, a veil that covers the hair and the neck. Others wore the *niqab*, which also covered the face, leaving a small horizontal slit through which only a woman's eyes were visible. The burka, on the other hand, completely obscured the face. I rarely saw the burka worn in Egypt except by complete paupers. To me, it seemed that conservative dress was a symptom of low socioeconomic class.

Men also dressed modestly. Almost never did I see an Egyptian man wearing shorts in public, and on the few occasions I wore shorts outdoors, I felt moderately uncomfortable. Although I never sensed scorn or noted a disapproving look, shorts were completely out of place. So I stopped wearing shorts even on the hottest days. Fortunately, my linen wardrobe helped mitigate the force of these social mores. In appearance and sensitivities, I had changed, and so too had Egypt. The phrases *abel el tharwa* ("before the revolution") and *bad el tharwa* ("after the revolution") preceded most explanations for changes following the events of January 25, 2011. The uprising was credited or blamed for just about everything during the two years I was in Cairo, which followed the uprising.

Why was traffic in Tahrir Square, a roundabout, sometimes moving clockwise when it had always flowed counter-clockwise? Because *bad el tharwa*, there were no traffic police officers.

Why were there periodic gasoline shortages and rolling blackouts that had never existed before the uprising? Because *bad el tharwa*, the good technocrats had been chased into exile or were too scared to join a government that might not endure.

Why were Egyptians protesting every minor social injustice? Why were workers endlessly striking? Why had traffic jams become even worse?

What followed the phrase "after the revolution" inevitably did not matter—every change seemed to exist because of the uprising. The events that began January 25 would change me, too, but those changes would take time to understand. In the meantime, I had a business to salvage.

11 BUMPING INTO A TERRORIST

I had resigned from my position at a prestigious Boston investment management firm to work full time on our Egypt fund. By the time I gave two weeks' notice of my departure, Howie and I had secured enough investor commitments to afford our planned Cairo operations and my full-time involvement. All that was left to do was to ink the internal agreement that governed my relationship to the fund and I would be "living the dream." I expected that I would be moving to Cairo soon.

By June of 2010, our partnership agreement was inked, and I was in New York's John F. Kennedy airport, headed to Egypt. In the airline lounge, I posted on Facebook that I would soon be in Cairo, half the world away, after flying the equivalent of 1.5 laps of the US. A friend posted what would turn out to be a prescient comment: "Be safe." Having purchased the obligatory four-bottle import allowance of Johnnie Walker Black Label scotch, the rarer ingredient in Egypt's national cocktail of soda water and scotch, I headed to the gate intending to board the plane early with other frequent flyers.

When I reached the gate, I found myself swarmed by an unwieldy queue. Well more than half an hour before the flight, passengers were jockeying for position near the jetway, as if seats would only be awarded to those first to board. I put this down to a cultural phenomenon: The magnitude of a line's disorder relates to a country's economic policy. Simply, more centralized (communist) economies create shortages, and the result is that people with reserved airplane seats feel compelled to jostle for boarding position just as they jostle for other goods that are frequently in short supply.

That night in the boarding lounge, a young Arab male with a particularly thick black beard bumped up against me twice. It was his overflowing camouflage backpack that kept hitting me. He was just like the beginner skier who, with his skies horizontal over his shoulder, carelessly rotates in a crowd, hitting others.

Just after the gate agent collected my ticket, I was moderately surprised to see four uniformed and armed immigration agents standing at the entrance to the jetway. My stomach turned when I moved further along and rounded the corner of the bridge. I began inventorying what I may have done to prompt this intimidating sight, thinking back to my first encounter with US Homeland Security, which had taken place a year earlier, when I still had my day job in Boston.

On that occasion, I had returned from Cairo, landing in New York, after using vacation time from my day job to further research our idea of investment in urban Cairo real estate. I had never before had a problem with US immigration officials, not even after returning from my trips to Yemen, but this time was different. Asked the purpose of my trip, I said, "Business," which prompted the armed agent to say that he could not process my passport at his station. He escorted me into a room with a one-way mirror, and I was left staring at my unshaven, travel-weary reflection.

Another passenger joined me in this holding area, an Arab man in his twenties. We were seated in front of a counter, behind which stood the agents who I assumed were to conduct the interrogations. The other man was questioned first, and the first question I heard was "Mohamed, are you going to be a good boy during your visit this time?" The question seemed patronizing to me, but I quickly intuited that he had a prior arrest in the United States. What was I doing in the same room as him?

I was asked for details about my business, such as the spellings of my partners' names and the name of our company. When asked for a business card, I must have displayed a level of unease. The only business card with my name on it was that of my Boston day job. The last thing I could possibly allow was for the federal government to call my current employer and ask about my "other" business in Egypt, as I had told nothing to my employer about the possibility that I might resign to manage a direct investment in Egypt.

For twenty minutes, a US immigration agent interrogated me. His Russian name and accent reminded me of the obligatory Russian KGB character in most spy movies. I figured they were suspicious for one of two reasons: Perhaps I had collectively made enough trips to the Mideast, including the increasingly hot spot of Yemen, to prompt a flag in their system, or they noticed that I had purchased a new ticket in Cairo when I changed my travel plans. Either way, the immigration agent would not tell me why I was on the list. I would be stopped and questioned on other entries to the United States, but this night in New York, boarding a flight to Cairo, I was worried when I saw the four immigration agents. When were people stopped from leaving America?

I whizzed by them as one of the first people to board, but when I stepped onto the jetway and turned the corner, twenty more agents, some plainclothes but all heavily armed, lined the corridor. Other passengers joked that perhaps there was a terrorist getting on board. In fact, there was.

When I landed in Egypt, I learned that an apparent terrorist had attempted to board my flight. I had the strangest feeling, as if I knew exactly who it was—he had been hitting me with that backpack, and his thick beard had given him a menacing look. Days later, press sketches would confirm my brush with a purported terrorist. A year later, he pled guilty to conspiring to murder individuals outside the US by trying to join a designated terrorist organization.

By now, such encounters were routine for investors in the Arab world. Months earlier, I had been slightly suspicious when I met with a small Egyptian law firm whose offices were in the same building in which a noted Egyptian dermatologist, Dr. Zawahari, practiced. I recognized the name immediately, and I later learned that the doctor was the brother of Ayman al-Zawahari, a top al-Qaeda militant[5] who, following the death of Osama Bin Laden, is believed to have assumed leadership of Al Qaeda. I was acutely aware that I was in close proximity to terrorists or their close family members.

The fund had been live for four months. I was working full-time in Egypt where my in-country role was to build financial models to determine prices we could offer for buildings, to brainstorm on negotiating strategy, and to be an information conduit to our limited partners, the passive investors. The problem was that I did not have much work after four months of operations in Egypt. After relying on local business consultants to take leadership responsibility for sourcing real estate properties, Howie changed strategy when he asked me to assume the in-country leadership role and to greatly increase the number of properties in our acquisition database. I would take on such a challenge and achieve his goal, but not before my frustration peaked when one of our senior consultants torpedoed a meeting that I felt would have greatly expanded our pipeline of potential investment properties.

There was a regularized apartment rental market in Downtown, and some rental listings were even written in English. Noting that two rental brokers had most Downtown listings, I requested a meeting with the one who had a fixed office. I figured that if the broker had access to apartments for rent, he would know landlords looking to sell their buildings and could solicit them for us.

One of our Egyptian consultants and I went to the meeting. The senior broker was admittedly a bit creepy. He was an Egyptian, thirty or so years old, and his shirt was unbuttoned to his midsection, with

---

[5] This was the relative mentioned by The New Yorker in its 2002 biography of infamous al-Qaeda leader Ayman Zawahari.

a rug of chest hair clambering its way to plain sight. His business partner looked emaciated. They were caricatures. We were seated at an angle of inferiority on stools so short they could have been ottomans.

I truthfully introduced our business concept to the brokers: We would buy rent-controlled buildings, pay tenants to leave, fix up the buildings, and re-rent them. I confided that we had not purchased a building and were seeking brokers who might know owners willing to sell. I cited their numerous listings of apartments for rent in buildings like those we sought to purchase. The hirsute one interrupted to ask what commission we would pay. We were prepared to pay 1.5 percent commission. I opened my mouth to announce the figure when our Egyptian consultant's torpedo hit me broadside. He responded to the broker's inquiry by saying, "Oh, we're not buying buildings now. We're just conducting market research on prices."

I was livid. Nothing could be further from the truth. We knew the broker did not have an inventory of buildings for sale. No one did. He certainly had no asking prices to divulge. Our consultant continued: "What can you show us? Then we'll discuss commission." That turned an excellent opportunity to expand our pipeline into a chicken-and-egg dilemma where we would not find resolution. These brokers would certainly not reach out to the building owners without being given a carrot, the commission rate. The meeting immediately turned into a stalemate. We were nearly half a year into our full-time operations, and business was stalled. There were few results of which to speak, our pipeline still nearly dry on a mid-December day when I assumed responsibility for the entirety of our Egyptian operations. That day was merely a month before the Egyptian uprising.

The first action I took was to implore each of our employees to contribute ideas on how to fix what in my opinion was our most critical problem, the dearth of properties that had been identified as available for sale. I had my own ideas, yet that was my management style. I preferred to have subordinates brainstorm ideas and implement them, as I felt that employees would take more ownership of "their" ideas.

As I had hoped, each of my employees immediately contributed ideas that helped to quickly expand our pipeline of potential property acquisitions. It had taken six months to find only a few properties with the use of Egyptians agents managing the endeavor. In contrast, Suzy and I, with the help of two young college graduates I hired, were able to expand our acquisition pipeline nearly tenfold in the same amount of time. Howie and I concluded from this experience that when making investments in a foreign country, the best strategy is to maintain day-to-day control of in-country operations rather than assign the responsibility to local managing agents.

As part of our investment plan, we needed to incorporate several new Egyptian companies. Fortunately, one of Egypt's economic liberalizations had simplified that process. We first needed to retain an auditor, since all Egyptian companies must be audited. I interviewed two firms. Each was associated with a separate international accountancy consortium whose members included firms in Europe and the US. I had hoped that their membership in these self-policing consortiums would result in a sufficient level of integrity, but I was wrong.

As I explained our business model to one auditor, he marveled at the plan but suggested we might need help from the government. I knew we would not, but I heard him out. He shocked me as he authoritatively declared that large investments like ours could be assured success. All we needed to do was calculate the projected profits from our project and then pay the Mubaraks five to seventeen percent, depending on the scope of the government's assistance. He corrected himself to say that we would not pay the Mubaraks directly, instead wiring money to an offshore account controlled by a man who was purportedly a close business associate of the Mubarak family. This happened two weeks before Egypt's uprising, when business associates of the Mubarak government would capture headlines. Within days following the start of the uprising, one such businessman was declared a fugitive from Egypt and was stopped in

Dubai, reportedly carrying $500 million.

The auditor's candor shocked me the most. Was this really how business was done in Egypt? I did not think much more of it, as their bid for auditing services was about six times more than what we had been previously paying. I selected another auditing firm, who had overseen a couple of rent-controlled property transactions. They accepted that I would set the fee for their auditing services, and I learned that was the best way to short-circuit price negotiations in Egypt. I merely explained the price I had paid elsewhere and stated that I already thought that price high but wanted better service. I then named my price, take it or leave it.

Being the director of an Egyptian company entitled me to a work permit. With the authorization to work, I was issued a residency visa. I was legit. In Egypt, a foreigner must declare his or her address. The first opportunity to do so is on the landing card one must complete and provide to an Egyptian immigration officer. I began to doubt that government officials actually checked the addresses when Wendy explained that she had several times given obviously fictitious addresses—"10 Downing Street" comes to mind. The one-stop shop at Egypt's investment authority really was the only stop I was obligated to make with respect to my residency visa. I had been required to present myself there each time I applied or renewed my visa, and I only needed to sign the application in person, as my lawyer's paralegal handled all the paper shuffling and an obligatory introduction to the police general whose decision it was to issue the visa. Albeit it a brief formality, presenting myself for this onceover by a senior police officer had proven memorable.

The police general had sat in an overly air-conditioned private office beside the coterie of bureaucrats who oversaw visas and work permits. The door to his office was manned by an aged junior deputy, and their appearances were in stark contrast. The police general's shoes were brilliantly shined, his pants and shirt crisply creased and proportionally fit to his svelte body. Conversely, the deputy had slovenly donned his black lace-up shoes, laces missing, and stood on folded-over heel cups as if they were bedroom slippers. The deputy's sidearm was oriented such that he needed to reach around his exceptional girth to draw it, and I wondered if he could even accomplish the cross-draw technique. His buttons—which had presumably been reinforced, or else I do not know how they could have handled the strain of his portly form—were undone to his chest. Both had cushy jobs, but only the deputy seemed happy about that.

Each year, the paralegal would usher me into the police general's office, place my application on the general's desk, and introduce me in Arabic. I would merely add *Messah el kheir* ("Good afternoon"). The general would acknowledge me with an unintelligible grunt, and he would always sign the paper that granted my visa and recorded my residential address.

As part of my new in-country responsibilities, I would need to hire and sometimes fire our Egyptian staff. In one case, an office boy was an average performer, but he was moody and lacked initiative. His legal status decided his fate, as his national identification card was expired and he refused to renew it. To continue employing him, we would have needed a legitimate ID. To explain why he refused to renew his identification card, we imagined he may have dodged Egypt's compulsory military service.

Egypt's employment laws were heavily skewed in favor of employees. The result was that many public- and private-sector employees worked on temporary contracts, renewable annually at the employer's discretion. I was surprised to learn some Egyptian firms required that employees, as a condition to an employment offer, sign an undated letter of voluntary resignation. I struggled with the ethical implications of this suggestion, so I never asked any of my employees to do this.

Under Egyptian law, a dismissed employee was entitled to severance equaling two months' salary for every year served. Our office boy had earned three months' salary as severance, and I offered him more than triple that amount: ten months' severance in return for his written, voluntary resignation. The language was specific, noting that he had received all monies due him. He accepted on the spot, so I was surprised when he returned a week after his dismissal, asking for more money and to rescind his resignation.

Greed transcends all cultures. In Egypt, it sure seemed to come in a form I had not experienced in America, where Ponzi schemes, falsified mortgage documents, and hacked credit card databases were common headlines. The saddest instance of Egypt's generosity-related greed happened during an evening out with some of my closest friends when we had chosen to dine at a restaurant housed on one of several boats permanently moored along the Nile.

Nora, John and I were walking to dinner when we were approached by a child who had been loitering near the boat's gang plank, begging for money. The child's hair was shaved to a short stubble, its feet shoeless and covered in dirt. The child asked for an Egyptian pound, seventeen American cents, and, in her always generous manner, Nora said, "You're too cute. I will give you more." The child smiled and said, "Okay." Nora dug into her purse and handed over an EGP 20 ($3.33) note, and she asked the child's name. The child responded, "Samea," a girl's name—she looked anything but a little girl, with her shaved hair.

That moment exemplified why I was fortunate to have lived in Cairo. Many of my closest friends, including Nora, held different views on life than I did. She was a social democrat, I a libertarian. In America, I had the luxury of surrounding myself with a social circle whose ideologies matched mine. Cairo broke me out. There, I realized the pleasure of having a friend whose values exposed me to new experiences, some of which challenged my values. In this case, I would have never given money to a begging child. Instead, I gave to the crippled, aged man who sold lemons outside Apperitivo. The economist in me assumed that money given to any beggar would encourage such behavior, and I did not want to see children begging. Their parents, I felt, should be doing the begging. Still, I believed my friend had likely relieved the young girl of her duties for the evening after meeting the quota to which she was likely subjected.

However, I was wrong. Samea was still begging hours later, when we departed the restaurant. This time, no one gave the child money.

12 OF COPYCATS, CUPCAKES, AND COUGHING

My first due diligence trip to Egypt was in March 2008. Five months later, we had incorporated an Egyptian company and planned to acquire and redevelop a pilot property. To my surprise, before year's end, I read in an Egyptian newspaper that another group was seeking to buy rent-controlled properties and redevelop them. Al-Ismaelia for Real Estate Investments had incorporated in February of 2008, six months before we had. By December 2010, they reportedly owned twenty unique, rent-controlled properties.

Thus, there were two investment groups working to restore rent-controlled properties in Cairo. One was my own, and the other was Ismaelia. News articles reported that Ismaelia's funds had come from Saudi Arabian and Egyptian investors. Conversely, our investors were entirely American. Not a single one of our eighteen investors spoke Arabic or had done much business in the Arab world. However, we were the ones who had decades of experience in rent-controlled real estate investments. Our business plans were not easily imitated. The amount of money required was the major obstacle, as both of our business models were capital intensive. We each had approximately $50 million to invest in our endeavors. Buildings were to be purchased, tenants paid to leave, and contractors compensated for rehabilitation of the properties. The redevelopment of rent-controlled properties in Egypt had never before been attempted on an institutional scale, and this fact served as a deterrent to copycats.

There were several hundred rent-controlled properties in Downtown. The combined investment capital of our two competing companies meant we could collectively address no more than ten percent of the market. For Downtown to be fully rehabilitated and the value of our investment to be maximized, we needed more competitors. We needed copycats.

In 2009, a year before we decided to raise an investment fund for our project, we began to learn more about Ismaelia. Building sellers or their financial advisors were informing us that Ismaelia was reportedly acquiring rent-controlled properties for EGP 1,800 to 2,000 per built square meter ($28 to $31 per square foot). That intelligence was critical. Now we knew where the market was priced. Then, in November 2009, little more than a year before the Egyptian uprising, Ismaelia announced plans to expand their operations. They wanted to acquire 150 thousand built square meters, which would more than double the amount of property under their ownership.

To do this, they sought to increase the amount of money in their project from $50 million to $140 million. Furthermore, news articles explained that Ismaelia's previous plans had been delayed by the global financial crisis. Now they were prepared to move forward with increased commitments from both existing and new shareholders. The swift pace of Ismaelia's acquisitions and moderately high acquisition prices confounded us for some time. Not long after we began our in-country operations, Ismaelia solicited us to be passive investors in their endeavor by making a capital investment in their company. However, that was not our model, as we were intent on maintaining hands-on control over operations.

At his invitation, I met with Ismaelia's managing director, and, after hearing his pitch, I politely declined to become a passive investor in their endeavor. He had chosen to meet at Estoril, a long-in-the-tooth restaurant in the heart of Downtown. The waiters' soiled outfits and missing teeth were apropos to the overall condition of the area. Downtown, more so than the other boroughs I knew in Cairo, had the highest density of *baladi* bars—Americans might call them "dive bars." It seemed to me as though Estoril was becoming one of these, save for the fact that they still offered traditional Egyptian fare.

After assuming responsibility for our in-country operations, I began speaking to everyone who might have been even remotely able to identify owners wanting to sell their buildings. The shotgun approach worked: Our first building was under agreement a few months later at a price lower than what we would have been willing to pay. I had also greatly expanded our pipeline of potential acquisitions. Our database of Downtown properties had expanded nearly tenfold from what had been less than ten viable properties in the first six months to more than one hundred properties by the time we reached our one-year anniversary. Properties under negotiation expanded sixfold. The numbers meant I was capturing a greater ratio of less ideal buildings, but this was to be expected. I was speaking to every potential source of properties: rental brokers, accountants, lawyers, and *bawaabs*. (I had hired two Egyptians to wander about town, asking at cafés and approaching building supervisors, *bawaabs*, about which properties could be for sale.)

One of the rental brokers with whom I immediately began working when I assumed in-country leadership duties went by his stage name, Tito. He was a musician who sang and played the oud, a short, bulbous instrument that looked a bit like a guitar. When he arrived at our office for an introductory meeting, I thought he had just walked off the set of *Dance Fever*. His tight synthetic black pants, white shirt unbuttoned to his midsection, torso-length hair, and shiny necklace were a bit off-putting. Downtown was just that type of place, a receptacle for characters like Tito. So I gave him a chance to which he eagerly responded. A few weeks later, Tito would be on the front lines of the uprising, shot by security forces during the Police Day protests on January 25, 2011. Fortunately, he survived. He proved to be one of the most prolific sources of properties for sale—and the only man I ever knew to wear pink pants in Cairo.

Like our rent-control investment strategy, in Cairo there was always two or more of any one business. For example, there are two Four Seasons hotels in Cairo, separated by a mere mile on opposite sides of the Nile. The hotel on the east shore has the more posh address, while the Four Seasons on the west shore offers views of the famed Giza pyramids on days when the air quality permits.

Fall was the worst season for air pollution. Farmers burned discarded rice stalks, which left smoke to linger for weeks downwind over Cairo. After any six-week stint in Cairo, I inevitably developed an irrepressible tickle in my throat, which made for a modest but persistent cough, symptomatic of having inhaled too much of Cairo's pollution. I tried to seek the fresh air of Europe or America every month or so, and my cough always cleared up after a week. Even Beirut and Beijing, where environmentalists claim air pollution is a paramount problem, were to me a breath of fresh air compared to Cairo.

The culprits of Cairo's air pollution were manifold. The worst industrial offenders were factories that burned fossil fuels, while the greatest transport-related air pollutant was diesel fuel. Diesel was also the mostly heavily subsidized fuel in Egypt. In Cairo's rural areas, daily refuse was piled along the main irrigation canals, and from time to time, I observed the smoldering remnants of garbage piles. Fire had rid residents of the accumulated waste but had filled the environment with ash and air pollutants. Even Mother Nature's sandstorms contributed to the choking air quality. Those came in winter and were best combated by wrapping a scarf over one's face to filter the sand out of inhaled air, while glasses kept the sand out of one's eyes.

The air pollution in Cairo was measured by the World Health Organization (WHO) as being nearly seven times worse than that in New York City. The WHO recommends an upper limit of twenty micrograms per cubic meter for air pollutants ten microns or smaller in size. (A human sneeze produces particles one to five microns in diameter.) In Cairo, pollutants ten microns in size or smaller are 138 micrograms per cubic meter, more than six times the recommended limit.

Worse was the soot. Several times a week, ash would land on my shirt. What looked like a fleck of dirt was not to be removed by the flick of a finger. If I did that, a gray streak was inevitably left across my shirt. Blowing off anything that looked to be dirt was a much better course of action, though doing so required breathing in even more of Cairo's polluted air.

I became used to the pollution, at least outdoors. However, indoor air quality was lacking, too. Cairenes were heavy cigarette smokers. Unlike in most countries, taxes leveled on cigarettes were very modest, a fixed tax of EGP 1.25 ($0.21) per pack plus a variable component of fifty percent of the retail price. Lesser brand cigarettes sold for about one dollar a pack, taxes included, while imported brands like Marlborough were three dollars a pack. Of all the restaurants I visited in Cairo, I only recall one as having a non-smoking section. Bars were worse—they were smoke-filled dens. Even if a bender erased memories of the previous evening, the night's smoke-filled atmosphere was certain to linger in one's clothes.

During my tenure in Cairo, *shisha* became an increasingly popular vice. Elsewhere, the water pipes used to smoke fruit-flavored tobacco were termed hubbly bubblies. Unfiltered, the water pipes were certainly worse for one's health than cigarettes could be. They had long been the purview of Egyptian men, though they were now popular with teenagers of both genders.

Not all of Cairo's air pollution was a byproduct of fossil fuel consumption. The fouling of air was sometimes intended. In America, I had grown accustomed to laundered clothes that smelled like—well, actually, they did not smell at all. My wife and I used fragrance-free detergent and rarely wore cologne or perfume, as the scents gave us headaches. Fragrances have even been named the allergen of the year by the American Contact Dermatitis Society. In

Cairo, the opposite was true: Egyptians demanded fragrance. Even facial tissues were scented. (I found "peach"-scented tissues to be the least offensive.) Whenever I sent my butler shopping, he was never able to find scent-free laundry detergent, which meant that I smelled like a jasmine flower on most days. In the end, one simply could not avoid pollution in Cairo, outdoors, indoors, or, as I saw it, in one's laundry detergent.

Precipitation in Cairo: sand

That Cairo had two Four Seasons hotels struck me as odd, as most every city around the world only had one. Only six cities out of the uber-luxury brand's eighty-four locations have two hotels, and of those cities, most are home to the world's greatest absolute wealth. They are cities like London, Los Angeles, Singapore, and Tokyo. Cairo did not belong in the group, so why were there two Four Seasons in Cairo? The answer could be found in the phenomenon of copycats. Egyptians had a proclivity for copying.

I lived on Gezira Island, a narrow sliver of land one and a half miles long and a half mile wide and situated in the middle of the Nile. My borough there was named El Zamalek and was home to 420 thousand people residing on the most expensive real estate in Cairo. Shops on the island catered to wealthy expatriates and Egyptians. There were only two liquor stores I knew of on the island, one of which was a restaurant that sold wine and beer as take-away. Both were strictly regulated. Yet for retail businesses, with no such regulatory barrier to entry, no sooner would one retail concept appear than it would be copycatted weeks later.

Next to my building was the third of four gourmet cupcake shops. All sprang up within months and were all within a five-minute walk of each other. Even before the case of the cupcake shops, copycatting had been evident in the proliferation of art galleries, Western-style coffee shops, and even gourmet soft-serve ice cream parlors. The phenomenon became even more pronounced post-uprising, when retailers exploited the caretaker government's neglect of zoning and health regulation enforcements. Yet the practice of copycatting went back decades, if not millennia. After all, every important person built a pyramid. In modern-day Egypt, however, most copycatting was for business purposes.

This sometimes led to violence. To understand how business disputes could become violent, one must first know about the Egyptian police force. I knew several Zamalek traffic policemen by name. I greeted them daily along Brazil Street, where I lived, whereas the police who guarded embassies near my apartment were assigned irregularly. The running joke was that the AK-47-toting boys who donned police uniforms and guarded the embassies usually did not know which country's embassy they guarded. I asked the guards periodically to see if the running joke was a wives' tale. Luckily, it was. They knew which countries' embassies they were guarding, and their answers were sometimes the only words I could understand in our conversations, their speech usually burdened by the heavy accent of rural Upper Egypt.

Embassy guards and police officers were transported to their posts in police vans. One such van could double as a paddy wagon, and that model multiplied following the uprising. Yet the most common form of police transport was a light-duty pickup truck with a wooden bench affixed lengthwise to the bed. I found the sight of eight armed policemen crouched in the rear of such a diminutive truck laughable until one pulled up to me after dark. I was in a part of town I did not often frequent, so I was relieved when he rolled down his window and merely asked for directions. *Directions?* I thought. *Are these not the guys I have to call in an emergency?*

The driver could not have been a day more than sixteen years old. He looked barely fourteen, and his hands grasped the top of the steering wheel as if he needed the high point as leverage to alternately swing from depressing the pedals and looking over the dashboard. He wanted to know how to get to the boroughs of Imbaba and Shubra, quite possibly two of the most well-known and largest districts in greater Cairo. The directions were easy for me to communicate in Arabic, and he kindly thanked me and went on his way. This exchange happened nearly two years after Egypt's uprising. I began to wonder if a police force could possibly be more incompetent.

Between undereducated embassy guards, the jovial policemen assigned to tackle the habitual double parking along my street, and the lost police driver, I had no personal reason to loathe them. Yet citizen journalists were using social media to frequently claim human rights abuses by the secret police and central police forces. The gravity of the abuses included murder and sodomy. Thus, during and after the uprising, police officers became the targets of abuse, so they hid in their stations for months.

The absence of police working their regular beats meant sidewalks and even traffic lanes became places to sell wares. Talaat Harb Street in Downtown was a most striking example. Come late afternoon, the two outer lanes of the three-lane road and adjacent sidewalks became filled with clothing racks and tables. Vendors touted inexpensive, imported, and usually fake goods. SpongeBob was apparently in high demand, and the copycats were all selling something SpongeBob related: clothing, posters, and toys.

The most entertaining of the post-uprising copycats were the teenage boys hawking imitation soccer—nay, football—jerseys. This must have been the occupation of the boys I began to see with increased regularity, with their slicked-back hair and tight jeans. Following the uprising, these greasers found means to purchase inexpensive Chinese motorcycles, which cost about $750. One Chinese cycle brand was Keweseki, a play on the Japanese Kawasaki brand, which meant copycatting was not the sole purview of Egypt.

Imitating the real brand, Kawasaki

Always two or three astride a single motorcycle, the teenage boys would cruise around town at late hours, ogling young ladies. I assumed the extra chrome and neon lights affixed to their rides were meant to attract the attention of the fairer sex or offset the emasculating, high-pitched, standard-equipment horns they frequently used. It was behavior that transcended nations and religion: boys out cruising to impress the girls.

They were ambitious, if their job performance was any measure. Several would man a single table piled high with a mixed mess of imitation polyester football jerseys. The shirts came in sealed plastic bags that made a remarkably loud sound when popped open with a slap between the hands. Up and down the street, hawkers' cries were interspersed by those frightening pops. By morning, the tables and clothing racks would disappear, the police back on the street.

What led to business-related violence was the competition between traditional retailers and street vendors who blocked storefronts while hawking goods. Some brick-and-mortar stores began closing in the evening, the time when most Egyptians shopped. The headache and clientele that came with the proliferation of street vendors must not have been worth staying open in the evening. In more than one instance, feuds that broke out in the absence of police led to guns being fired.

The copycats were usually quite good, like the fake Nike store in Downtown. When my wife visited Cairo, I took her to a store I knew sold fake designer handbags. That day, an Egyptian police officer and the shop's owner were huddled in the back of the store, watching a parliamentary debate. In a shop full of counterfeit goods, the irony was not lost on me.

13 ILLICIT DRUGS ARE UNPATRIOTIC...
UNLESS WE GROW THEM

Every country has bureaucrats. India's are notorious. There, the post-British regime has been described as a License Raj, where an excessive number of bureaucratic procedures drives many to operate in the informal economy. In contrast, Estonia's paper pushers are efficient. In that Baltic bureaucracy, many procedures are completed online. In Egypt, the bureaucrats were reliably maddening but often comedic enough that I welcomed the opportunity to appear before them.

During a brief visit home to the US, I went to the cathedral of American bureaucracy, the Department of Motor Vehicles. I wanted to renew my car's registration. Three trips, two phone calls, and several hours resolved a modest automobile tax that had gone unpaid in my absence from America. If America only had one such dreadful bureaucracy, Egypt had dozens.

Egyptian bureaucrats were best at ginning up new procedural obstacles to what one wanted to accomplish. With a bit of patience and expended effort, the obstacles were surmountable. However, there were also times that nothing could be done to avoid the madness of bureaucracy. Egypt definitely had no monopoly on the inane, but it was expert at creating inanities.

Amongst my friends who were privately employed, few had work permits that allowed them residency visas. Yet all were common-law residents in Egypt. They were constructively employed and contributed to the national economic output. None were on the dole. They also consumed well more than the average Egyptian, further stimulating the local economy. For every economic reason, Egypt should have wanted these foreigners to remain in Egypt. In that matter, I learned that pure economic reasoning eventually triumphs, but not without misguided socioeconomic policies causing a fright.

Of the foreigners I knew who were not employed by foreign governments or multinational companies, most had been residing in Egypt for years on successively issued three-month tourist visas that could be purchased for fifteen dollars at the airport. Exiting every three months was not always a practical or financially possibility, so one's tourist visa could be extended for a small fee and a half-day spent at the Mugamma, a monolithic building in Tahrir Square that housed innumerable bureaucrats. Friends without the temperament to face the bureaucracy simply overstayed their visas and paid a fine when exiting Egypt. The largest fine of which I heard was EGP 150 ($30) for overstaying a tourist visa by six months, but suddenly, following the uprising, several policy changes threatened those foreigners who had called Egypt home for years but never properly obtained a residency visa.

Egypt's work permit and visa system were broken, evidence of poor economic policy and lax law enforcement. "Tourists" could overstay their visas for a nominal fine and work informally. I did not know any of these habitual tourists to be manual laborers, as Egypt had enough unskilled labor. Rather, the foreigners I knew who worked illegally included an investor relations professional, an entrepreneur with a garment business, a private school teacher, and a journalist for an English-language newspaper, the state-owned *El Ahram*. These "tourists" were not paying income taxes, and it may have been true that they were taking the jobs of equally capable Egyptians. Regardless, as the economy stalled following the uprising, the Egyptian government announced that tourist visas would not be renewed. There were soon stories that foreigners with many tourist visas in their passports were being refused re-entry.

Even those foreigners working for multinationals with valid work permits found themselves under pressure. The law required that Egyptian companies had no more than one foreign employee for every nine Egyptian employees. In some circumstances, that rule had been waived for the largest of multinationals with an understanding that the above-quota foreign employees would be temporarily resident while they trained Egyptians to assume the often middle-management duties the foreigners were assigned. When the foreigners in such circumstances repeatedly renewed their visas, the post-uprising caretaker government announced they would take action. In the end, the status quo would remain, but not before a few days of inanity, which would mean disaster for the tourism industry.

In the wake of the uprising, the Egyptian government announced a change to the visa policy. Tourists now needed to obtain visas prior to arriving at the Cairo airport. Officials characterized this policy change as a security measure to reduce the chance that terrorists would enter Egypt during the post-uprising instabilities. Fortunately, the new policy lasted no more than a couple of weeks before it was shelved. Having not heard of any tourists being turned away upon arrival, I suspected that the regulation had never been implemented. Meanwhile, policy reversals were becoming increasingly common in post-uprising Egypt. The caretaker government would announce new policies only for the bureaucrats not to enact them. Such were the conditions for doing business in Egypt. There were plenty of existing policies and new changes, but one never knew exactly which would be applied. However, the HIV test prerequisite to a residency visa was never overlooked, and this meant that Egypt's bureaucracy sometimes hurt, literally.

In Egypt, foreigners who are awarded a residency visa must be free of the human immunodeficiency virus (HIV). The lethargic pace of the government's visa office meant I was tested at least six times for the virus, more than twice the required number of tests. Once, while awaiting the renewal of my residency visa, I informed my lawyer of my travel plans. She had been holding on to my passport for a couple of weeks, shepherding it through numerous procedures. Relinquishing my passport to her was always a bit unnerving. Worse, the final procedure involved leaving my passport overnight at the government visa office, which, like most government offices I had visited, was littered with stacks of papers.

My lawyer cautioned that if I was to travel outside of Egypt before the bureaucracy had reviewed my blood test result and issued my visa, I would need to take another HIV test upon my return. The implication was clear. While low by international standards, an estimated population of ten thousand Egyptians did have HIV, a fact the Egyptian government seemed to ignore as the Egyptian policy assumed there was no probability that I could catch the blood-borne virus inside Egypt while awaiting the issuance of the residency visa. However, a single trip outside of Egypt while I was awaiting my residency visa meant I might be exposed to HIV, requiring a new blood test.

Egypt's socialized healthcare system was third rate. Wealthy Egyptians travelled to Europe or America for elective surgeries and treatments of chronic conditions, and even Mubarak's in-country attending physician was a German national whose intercontinental flight had brought new meaning to the term "house call." Egypt did have private hospitals and clinics, which were the best bet for time-sensitive procedures, like broken bones and heart attacks. That was to say, they were the best option for those who could make it to the hospital in a timely manner. I rarely saw ambulances, and when I did, they were never moving with any haste, just making lots of noise and sitting in traffic. Taking the nearest taxi to a private hospital was the recommended course of action in an emergency.

I had no reason to fret the result of the blood test until I learned that the hepatitis C virus (HCV) affected ten to thirteen percent of Egypt's population. That was the highest rate of HCV incidence in the world and more than ten times the rate of infection in the US.

The pernicious virus is the leading cause of liver cirrhosis and liver cancer in Egypt and one of the top five causes of death. The initial conveyance of the disease was due to inadequate needle hygiene during nationwide vaccination treatment programs. Reuse of needles had been a necessity because syringes were made of glass during that period, which lasted from the 1960s to the 1980s. Reused needles were often inadequately sterilized, according to one report, because of the time constraints of using boiling water. Until the mid-1990s, the disease continued to spread through blood transfusions, so when it came time to have my blood drawn as a prerequisite to my residency visa, I took extra precaution, choosing a private nurse.

I had been an emergency medical technician for a number of years, so I recognized that his needles' sterilization seals were intact. As well, he used spring-loaded retracting needles, which meant that when the draw of my blood was complete, the needle would retract into a protective sleeve, preventing the nurse from accidentally pricking himself and prohibiting the reuse of the needle. Still, I was always a bit nervous before the test results. Egypt's HCV history kept me that way, and so too did an American Embassy policy that highlighted the shortcomings of Egypt's healthcare system.

A friend of mine, who worked at the US Embassy in Cairo, explained a policy I never confirmed, though it made perfect sense: Whenever an American citizen working at the US Embassy was admitted to a hospital in Egypt, he was to notify the embassy. In certain cases, the embassy would send a medical officer to monitor the treatment. In a case my friend explained, the Egyptian medical staff was attempting to administer expired medicine, and the medical officer caught the mistake. Purportedly, expired medicines were common in Egyptian hospitals, so when articles about the government's medical policies made it into the press, I took notice. One story about drugs, the illicit type, gave me a great laugh.

I was not sure who the Egyptian leviathan rewarded—certainly not efficient paper-pushers or contemplative reasoners. When reasoning was expected of a bureaucrat, one would inevitably read an interview as nutty as the one with Bahaa Zoheir, the commanding officer of Egypt's Anti-Narcotic General Administration. The article appeared in the *Egypt Independent* on July 26, 2011, entitled "Legalizing drugs in Egypt: Just a pipe dream?" though it should have been titled "Illicit drugs are unpatriotic unless grown in Egypt." An abridged outline of the commanding officer's views follows.

On the law, broadly: "There is no way hashish, or any other drug will ever be legalized in Egypt, nor should it be."

Reason One: "We are living in an Islamic society, with traditions and beliefs that must be preserved."

Reason Two: "It's the role of the state to protect the individual from his or her self. If that's the case, then how could I possibly allow them to take drugs and harm themselves in that way?"

Reason Three: Consuming or trafficking drugs is a "highly unpatriotic practice."

On tax policy and due process: "Who needs taxes? When we arrest drug users or dealers, we take their stuff anyway."

On import policy: "If this stuff was grown in Egypt, then maybe it might have some kind of economic benefit, but the climate here does not permit the growth of good-quality cannabis and opiates. All you get is low-quality stuff."

I never tired of the hilarious statements often made by Egyptian government officials. What bureaucrats told me in private conversation would not be believable unless such absurdities had been regularly documented in the local press. Fortunately, the brightest government officials recognized this inanity and admitted to it.

14 NEGOTIATIONS

Egypt is its famed Khan el Khalil market, the entire country a bazaar. Most everything, save prepared food and groceries, is negotiated in Egypt. In Cairo, my responsibilities included negotiating building acquisitions and professional services. With some patience, one discovers Egypt has three price levels: fresh-off-the-plane foreigner, resident foreigner, and Egyptian.

Fresh-off-the-plane prices apply to tourists and some multinational executives. Whether for cheap Chinese-made souvenirs or employee salaries, the price paid by these uninformed consumers is easily twice what can be negotiated. These easy marks find satisfaction with their transaction price since most everything in Egypt is cheaper than in the developed world. Furthermore, anything with a material component of labor is shockingly inexpensive.

As a rule, I paid my Egyptian staff well above market salaries once a new hire demonstrated he or she was competent. Most do not so prove themselves. "Well above market" could be confused with sweatshop wages until one realizes forty percent of Egyptians live on less than two dollars a day. I paid my least-skilled employees nearly six times the poverty rate and multiples of what the Egyptian government usually paid for equivalent work.

As a military school graduate, I polish my shoes weekly in the US. At $0.49 for a proper shoeshine in Egypt, the price is a remarkable ninety percent lower than a shine in Boston's financial district. A just-off-the-plane foreigner would have been happy to pay $1 or $1.50 for a shoe shine. This is the trick to price discrimination in Egypt. When I was paying the resident foreigner price of $0.49 for a shoe shine, I was paying fifty percent more than was paid by Egyptians. Such was the ability for even a shoeshine boy to price discriminate. No matter how hard I tried to pay a lower amount, one matching that paid by Egyptians, protestations would guilt-trip me into paying a premium over the local price.

With a little effort, discovering the resident foreigner price level is easy. Whatever price is asked by the Egyptian seller is the just-off-the-plane price. Ignore it, but first, find yourself some friends. My expatriate friends willingly compared notes on negotiable goods, like apartment rents and taxi fares. For labor prices, Mohamed El Sewedy, the Egyptian businessman whom I had known since we were polo teammates at boarding school, was my touchstone. Never did I make a salary proposal without first asking him.

At the airport, one needs a negotiating strategy to deal with all the taxi solicitors. I found the most effective negotiating tactic was to introduce competition, a bidding war. By simultaneously negotiating with several hawkers, competition erupts, leading to the market price, about EGP 50 ($8.33). Negotiations generally started at twice that amount.

In one experience, my bargaining was not over when I reached a modestly below-market price. I was to suffer a new ruse. Having gone to the airport parking lot and loaded my luggage and me into his taxi, the taxi driver asked that I wait a moment. I thought the driver was going to deliver a message to a friend or give a bribe to a policeman monitoring his presence. (Taxis are required to buy a special permit to pick up airport passengers, and I suspected my driver had not done so.) After some time, I grew frustrated and moved my luggage into a neighboring taxi. No sooner had I closed the car door than the first driver came running, shouting. He had corralled another passenger and was upset at the other driver for scooping me. I imagined he had gone into the arrivals hall and immediately underbid others, figuring two below-market passengers would amount to a single above market fare. Clever, I thought. Had he started his car and air conditioning while I was waiting for him, I might have been comfortably duped.

Deciphering price levels was important for day-to-day life. However, a completely different negotiating problem would be a major obstacle to our business: Egyptians had no idea what their buildings were worth. The problem was asymmetric information, and I, the foreigner, held that information. Egyptians are suspicious of foreigners, and there was even a slang term for us: *khawaga*. The moderately derogatory term means "master" and was used to describe not only non-Egyptians but also Egyptian Jews in the gold business. Xenophobia and prejudices were not recognizable in casual interactions with taxi drivers or waiters, but candid conversation with an Egyptian will demonstrate they view Palestinians as too crafty to be trusted; Nubians, the dark-skinned Egyptians from Upper Egypt, as uneducated; and Gulf Arabs as upstarts to be disrespected, undeserved of their oil wealth and haughty attitudes.

With money to spend buying old buildings in Cairo and the asymmetric knowledge of a building's potential profitability, I was a *khawaga*, a clever outsider. Building sellers feared that I was to be their "master." They thought I would purchase their buildings for an amount much less than fair market value and make an immediate profit, and this fear sometimes proved to be excruciatingly difficult to alleviate.

I would liken it to a situation in which a white man comes into an Egyptian home and admires an heirloom painting that is prominently displayed. The Egyptian owner has certainly been told by his parents that the painting is the family's most valuable asset. In this situation, I would be the sharp *khawaga*, standing in the living room and offering to buy it as though I were a Sotheby's expert. Inevitably, the Egyptian would start the negotiation with an obscene asking price, no different than if he was asking me to pay twenty dollars for a two-dollar tchotchke.

The seller of a rent-controlled building could never name any economic reason for his high asking price. He was not embarrassed about this, either. In one instance, the owner of a building asked EGP 40 million ($6.67 million), though the property produced a mere EGP 720 thousand ($120 thousand) of income per year. I would often demonstrate that this type of building had only a 1.8-percent yield (income divided by building price) when Egyptian bank deposits were paying ten percent annually. In developed markets like America or Europe, real estate yields should be higher than the yield on a bank savings account, meaning this particular building should have been priced at no more than EGP 7.2 million ($1.2 million), more than eighty percent lower than the seller's asking price. For this property, our offered price would eventually reach EGP 21.3 million ($3.55 million). Our belief that we could pay many tenants to leave and complete a restoration of the property to dramatically raise rents was implied in our willingness to accept a yield much lower than that of a bank account. Still, if a deal was to be consummated, the seller would have to reduce his asking price by fifty percent.

The protection that building ownership offered against the intermittent depreciations of a Third-World currency weakened my bank-deposit argument. After traveling across emerging markets and learning that building yields were consistently lower than I had expected, I understood that real estate was considered a better store of wealth than a bank deposit. Perhaps that was the reason that only ten percent of Egyptians held bank accounts.

A chance conversation in Lebanon in October 2011 would solidify my understanding of the role real estate plays in the Third World. I had been invited to Beirut to deliver a lecture, "Financial Turmoil and the Arab Spring." During lunch, a Syrian professor could not be tempted to forecast political developments, as she knew there could be consequences for doing so. Assad was still firmly in power, though he faced a growing rebellion. What she did explain was that Syrians were not allowed to hold foreign currency, that a black market for the Syrian pound had developed, and that apartments and houses were being snatched up. The implication was that Syrians were worried about a currency devaluation. Debasement was a regular occurrence in other countries that had experienced civil war. Incoming regimes would often fail to honor the debts of previous regimes, sometimes by printing money to monetize the debt. This explained why real estate prices were actually rising in Syria even though the death toll was also rising. This meant that inhabitants of emerging markets knew the likelihood of inflation much better than I did. Later, our first deal would be scotched in part when the seller decided, "Egyptian pounds in the bank are worthless compared to a building on the ground."

Other sellers were just plain greedy. Such was the case in the few instances when the seller had recently acquired a building. A stark example was an empty building on Mohamed Mahmoud Street. The building stood opposite the mothballed American University in Cairo (AUC) downtown campus and had been sold eighteen months earlier for EGP 3.2 million ($530 thousand). I knew this because I had been introduced to the seller's accountant who credibly volunteered the EGP 3.2-million amount and was incredulous when I told him the seller was asking for EGP 7 million ($1.17 million), as a purchasing price of EGP 3 million ($500 thousand) would have justified our investment. Needless to say, the seller was greedy in his attempt to double his money in little more than a year.

On occasion, I tried copying Egyptian negotiating tactics. Once I used a walk-out strategy to intimidate a building owner while negotiating to acquire his property. Others had tried the tactic on me. It worked for me, as I dismissed his counteroffer by immediately leaving the meeting, and he chased me to the elevator and further lowered his price.

I had also learned that the negotiation experiences we were having were common in Egypt. The nascent market for rent-controlled property was like a Turkish carpet bizarre, where asking prices were ridiculously high. For example, one building in Downtown had purportedly been purchased for EGP 23.5 million ($3.92 million). The buyer explained negotiations had started with the owner demanding EGP 60 million ($10 million) to which he countered with an offer of EGP 12 million ($2 million). The deal concluded when the seller reduced his price by more than sixty percent.

Whether we asked a seller's price or offered our price first, asking prices were nearly all stratospheric. For a building near the Egyptian stock exchange, we offered EGP 6 million ($1 million). I was negotiating with two recent college graduates who were handling their family's ownership of the building, and their technique was to preemptively shift the insanity of their counteroffer to a third party. They were too bright to demand such an obviously above market price, so they countered my offer and declared that a friend felt the building was worth EGP 30 million ($5 million). I walked away without even making a counteroffer. When the broker restarted the negotiation months later, he communicated an ingeniously veiled counteroffer. The broker explained that a different buyer had been found who was willing to pay EGP 12 million ($2 million) and that an independent appraisal had established the building's value at EGP 18 million ($3 million), so that was their counteroffer: EGP 12 million. We declined, and they still owned the building as of publication of this book.

I found it necessary to explain our business model to sellers: Acquire, negotiate for tenants to leave, renovate, and re-lease. Otherwise, they would have been suspicious of my motivations in buying their buildings. Sellers would then estimate the renovated value of the building and subtract costs of tenant key money, the amount paid to vacate a tenant, and renovation. The remainder was what the seller demanded for his building, and this meant the seller allowed no profit between my combined costs and the expected sale value of a renovated building.

During a brief respite in the United States, episodes of the

American television show Pawn Stars gave me solace, as Americans did the same sort of negotiation when pawning items. In some cases, the pawn shop owner would have asymmetric information, when he knew the true retail value of the item being offered for pawn or sale. For the benefit of the show's viewers and the item's seller, an independent expert would appraise the item and declare the retail value to the pawn shop owner and the seller. What inevitably happened next was what struck me as familiar: The seller would announce an asking price equivalent to the item's retail value, overlooking the marketing and overhead expenses that the pawn shop seller would incur to subsequently liquidate the item. For example, the retail value of a rare guitar would be declared as five thousand dollars, and the seller would ask for that amount, implying that the pawn shop owner was entitled to a grand profit of zero when he later sold it. Genuine sellers would settle for approximately half the item's retail value, which was usually the pawn shop's maximum offer. Sellers of buildings in Downtown similarly needed to accept a cut of fifty percent or more to the renovated value and the net of tenant and restoration costs. The fact that I, as an investor, was entitled to make a profit was usually conceded by sellers, but grudgingly.

Contrary to the situation in Pawn Stars, there were no truly independent appraisers in our business even though, in the late 2000s, a board of property appraisers had been formed in Cairo. During our foray into the market, there were 120 certified appraisers. None I met knew anything about historic rent-controlled properties, and their appraisal methods were irrelevant. First, the replacement value method was meaningless, as no one could be found to build high-ceiling ornate properties with exquisite finishing as they had done in the early twentieth century, nor could many of the materials be sourced. With little cash flow from deeply discounted controlled rents, a discounted cash-flow model made no sense, either. Comparable sales would be the only moderately applicable method.

More disturbing was my realization that appraisers were enabling

Egyptian banks to conceal losses and financial companies to overstate assets. In one instance, I had taken an interest in an ideal property located near the stock exchange. The building's vacant floors had been the headquarters of a now defunct company, and they must have been vacant for some time. Purportedly for sale by a state-owned bank, the floors of empty apartments were reminiscent of the moon's surface, covered in thick dust and absent footprints. No one had inspected the property in years, and the other units were still rent controlled. I thought the negotiation would be easier as the seller was a financial institution and should have known the fair market value of its assets. I was wrong.

I offered EGP 11.5 million ($1.9 million) and was prepared to pay upwards of EGP 14 million ($2.33 million), but I had allowed room for counteroffers. The price was a premium valuation since seventy percent of the building's apartments were empty, and this saved me the expense of paying tenants to vacate the property.

The firmness of the bank's response was uncharacteristic for Egypt. The bank countered with a firm EGP 18 million ($3 million), not a pound less. The bank's "independent" appraiser had valued the building at EGP 18 million, but in a candid discussion with the bank officer, we learned that the appraiser's EGP 18-million valuation had been identical to the principal value of a defaulted loan that the building had secured. This was no coincidence. The building was part of a fraud, and there was no way it could ever be worth EGP 18 million.

I would see this same kind of fraud in three separate instances. I figured the scheme worked like this: A loan would inevitably have been written quite a few years earlier (in the above case, ten years earlier). At that time, a building would be put up as collateral, valued by a bank officer as being well above its fair market value. In the examples I knew, the borrower defaulted quickly, leaving the bank with insufficient collateral, an over-appraised building.

Most banks were owned by the government. Their employees had secure but low-paying positions, even the executives. Two possibilities explained why a bank would underwrite an under-collateralized loan that would quickly go into default: Either the loan officer was grossly incompetent, or he was an accomplice to a fraud. I suspected the latter, as that officer would likely be given a sizeable kickback by the borrower. Regardless, how the bank handled the default would affect my ability to buy the building, as the bank could perpetuate the fraud by never valuing the building to market.

Normally, when a bank forecloses on assets, those assets are appraised. Any appraised value less than the loan's outstanding principal should be recorded as a loss. In the instance of this building, which housed a defunct company's headquarters, I estimated that when the bank had foreclosed nearly ten years earlier on the property, the sole collateral to the EGP 18-million loan, the building had easily been worth less than EGP 10 million ($1.67 million). The bank should have reported to its shareholders a loss of at least EGP 8 million ($1.33 million), but I suspect it had not done so. With enough—or perhaps any—losses, the bank manager would be sacked or sent to a branch in rural Egypt. That was why the bank would insist on a sale price well above fair market value and equivalent to the loan's principal value. There was no other rational explanation when one considered the bank's opportunity cost of continuing to hold the building.

In this example, the building was producing EGP 336 thousand ($56 thousand) of annual income, equivalent to a yield of about 2.9 percent based on my proposed purchasing price of EGP 11.5 million ($1.92 million). By refusing my offer, the bank was rejecting a fifteen-percent yield on short-term government bonds. The bank's opportunity cost was nearly EGP 1.4 million ($230 thousand) of annual income, which it was happy to forgo. Why, though? The only answer was so that they could avoid recording a loss on the loan.

The appraiser's role in the ongoing fraud was to collect a fee from the bank and provide an independent valuation that, remarkably, was not only well above market prices but also identical to the loan's defaulted value. I imagined the skeletons I would find if I could be put in charge of a state-owned bank. Months later, I met the chief financial officer of a privatized bank who was in just such a position. He said that when the formerly state-owned bank had been acquired by his employer, EGP 4 billion ($670 million) of the EGP 4.4 billion ($770 million) in loans was in default. When he and his colleagues reported material losses, Egyptians who had remained minority shareholders complained about his team's horrible management. The previous management team, having been Egyptian government employees, had not lost money. No, they had just covered up a large number of frauds.

Some negotiations resulted immediately in lost propositions. One evening, I was with John Harris as he parallel parked on a public street. As he locked the car and we walked away, an Egyptian came over, waving what looked like a booklet of parking tickets and speaking in Arabic. He pointed to an official-looking ID that hung from a string necklace and said he was responsible for collecting parking fees. This was after the January 25 uprising, but street parking was still free. We knew immediately that he was conning us, but my friend's car was at risk of being vandalized if we did not pay. There were no police officers in sight, as had been the case before the uprising. John gave him EGP 5 ($0.83), and the purported "official parking manager" did not bother to write us an official receipt. In fact, he probably could not write.

Outside the market for rent-controlled real estate, there were examples of even greater differences between prices asked by buyers and sellers. A dramatic example was the case of striking transportation drivers, who demanded an adjustment to their retirement bonuses. They had been entitled to receive three months' salary equivalent as a bonus. Their demand? Nearly three thousand percent higher. They wanted a retirement bonus equal to one hundred months' salary. Egypt was a bazaar, even for Egyptians.

Other conversations, like employee reprimands, somehow turned into a negotiation. When managing my Egyptian staff, I had learned that reprimands needed to be preceded by offering a way to save face, or else the person being reprimanded would dispute the facts or focus on trying to shift the blame. The best tactic was to shift the blame ahead of time so that future expectations could be the substantive point of a reprimand. The negotiating part of the reprimand came in getting the employee to accept the manufactured cause for his or her poor performance with the employee attempting to assign the blame on someone else or me. When an Egyptian employee was quite late to a meeting, I excused him because of the traffic. Then I told him I would buy him a cheap watch and he would leave his house earlier, no excuses. When a real estate agent did not communicate the correct terms of my purchase offer, I started the reprimand by blaming myself for the miscommunication, even though I had not been responsible for the oversight, nor had I miscommunicated to my agent. After blaming myself, I told the agent he had to repeat to me the terms whenever he was going to make an offer. Sometimes, we even role-played. Had I not assigned blame to someone or something else, reprimands would have been taken as an insult, a direct accusation of incompetence, and that sort of thing is not done in the Arab world.

Even senior executives in Egypt had the habit of shirking responsibility. In one instance, a service provider with whom we were negotiating claimed a junior lawyer had advised him that the best negotiating tactic was to walk out of the meeting and refuse to participate in any dialog. When explaining his actions, the executive placed blame on a junior lawyer for suggesting such a disruptive tactic. My time spent in the Middle East allowed me, in hindsight, to understand the situation—in Egypt and Yemen, rarely would anyone accept responsibility for an obviously poor decision.

15 POLO AMIDST A REVOLUTION

I was in Dubai the week before the Police Day protests, which began on January 25, 2011. Eighteen days later, those same protests would topple President Hosni Mubarak. In the meantime, John, Mohamed, another Gezira Club teammate and I had travelled to the Emirates for a two-day polo match. The polo field was the centerpiece of a Dubai housing development and was used frequently during Dubai's temperature-shortened seasons. The United Arab Emirates, I was told, were scorching hot for much of the year. However, a Yemeni friend residing in Dubai had explained to me that the heat was manageable: One simply needed to drive from air-conditioned garage to air-conditioned garage, never stepping foot in the sweltering heat.

From what I could see, there were not enough people in the city of Dubai. Recently constructed houses and apartment buildings were devoid of inhabitants. At the polo field, villas were erected but incomplete, casualties of the property market collapse. Elsewhere in Dubai, artificial islands formed in the shape of the continents had attracted only speculative interest. No one had built there, and now the islands were reportedly sinking before anything except a model house could be built.

Both planned polo games were rained out, a rarity in Dubai, so we did the unthinkable: We went skiing in a mall in the desert. At the Mall of the Emirates, a ski slope with 250 feet of vertical drop had been constructed. Knowing the local market, the mall's owners catered to the large expatriate population, who craved the environmental equivalent of comfort food: snow. Some guests were there to carve several consecutive turns before riding the lift back to the top. More people, mostly children, were there just to frolic in the snow. A pass to the chairlifts and ski equipment was priced only moderately higher than access to the base area, where children played in the snow as if they had never before seen it. This was probably true, as most appeared to be the offspring of guest workers from snowless climates. Skiing in the desert would be the first of several seemingly incongruous experiences over the coming months, though these circumstances would not really come to an end until I left Egypt and the project two years later.

The surreal situations began with the Police Day uprising. Police Day was a national holiday to celebrate the societal contributions of the national police force, though in 2011, the irony of the event was not lost on a citizenry who loathed the force's penchant for brutality. Days earlier, a courageous twenty-six-year-old Egyptian woman named Asmaa Mahfouz had posted a provocative and declarative statement on YouTube[6] announcing her intentions to participate in the January 25 demonstration and calling on others to join her. The number of dissidents who assembled in Tahrir Square to protest police brutality surprised everyone, as did the events that followed.

I, however, had a polo game to play. On January 25, my Gezira Sporting Club polo team played a practice match. We were preparing to defend our league championship. Our best competition? The police force's polo team.

"The game of kings," as polo is described, was played by armed civil servants in Egypt, not by kings. The police also fielded teams in more proletariat sports, like soccer and basketball, but they were

---

[6] This video can be found at www.youtube.com/watch?v=SgjIgMdsEuk.

rarely at the top of the league standings. Polo was a different story. It was a serious undertaking for the police force, unlike the enforcement of traffic regulations. I knew this firsthand, as I had been drafted months earlier by Gezira's team to play in the previous season's decisive fall match.

Egypt's national polo league consisted of three sporting clubs and the police. Our Cairo-based team was stabled at the prestigious sporting club built by the British during their occupation, though the club's nationalization under Gamal Abdel Nasser had deeply scarred its then world-renowned polo facilities. All three full-size fields had been seized and repurposed, some portion used to form a "people's" sporting club. Today, the grounds are barren fields of dirt that barely resemble their intended use as soccer pitches.

Gezira club polo players still kept their ponies at the club and had an area to individually practice. I was fortunate to live within walking distance and could have practiced daily, though I did not, as our investment efforts consumed most all of my weekday time. On the days I was free, the practice fields were occasionally under water, the result of a lazy watering technique. Rather than water regularly, the club's staff simply rolled an open-ended hose onto the field and turned it on until the area was soaked in standing water.

In that decisive fall 2010 game against the police, we were pitted against a police force general, a colonel, and two younger players. I was meant to be the worst player on the field, as evidenced by my minus-one handicap. That day, my performance was that of a "ringer," a player whose handicap is advantageously too low. No one in Egypt knew me, and I had hardly played polo since fifteen years earlier at Cornell University. Thus, Gezira was able to convince the Egyptian Polo Federation to give me a very low handicap, that of a new player. We won that day, but not before I was subjected to some of the most unsportsmanlike polo ever.

Early in the game, the umpires summarily removed the police team's general, who had loudly disputed a call. The umpires conversed with Farouk, who was overseeing the match at his field, and eventually reinstated the general to the match. Later, I learned just how important this match was. The police team turned, well, brutal.

I was injured midway through the match, having collided with another player at an awkward angle that crushed my knee between horses. At the chukker's intermission, I dismounted to change horses and could not put any weight on my injured leg. Though I told our team captain that I could not continue, I succumbed to peer pressure and reentered the match, cheered on by teammates.

The police team's colonel had so far been a polite but competitive player in the match. Off the field, he was a jovial man whom I bumped into at the Gezira club on occasion. I liked him. When he asked, "Which leg did you hurt?" I responded in jest and said, "I'm not telling you. You might aim for it."

He said, "No, really, I want to know so I don't hurt it."

I admitted, "It's my left leg."

The general must have overheard, as no sooner did we restart with the first gallop down the field than he directed his horse straight for my injured leg. The crushing force of his horse against my knee hurt horribly. Such was polo. The sport was full contact, but I questioned his sportsmanship. Though the hit was fair, it was unnecessary for the type of play in which we were involved. I limped for several weeks and was sidelined from polo for two months. That we won the match was infinitely gratifying. Only afterward did I learn that the police had gone home poorer than they had expected, having earned no bonus for losing, and I experienced a momentary feeling of schadenfreude.

Months later, I witnessed a similar callousness by the police, beginning on Tuesday, January 25, 2011. That day began innocuously, with Cairo's streets relatively empty, much like they would have been on a Friday morning, when Egyptians slept in prior to attending noon-hour prayers at their local mosques.

No sooner had we finished the polo scrimmage on January 25 than players immediately checked their smartphones. The habit was pervasive in Egypt, where checking one's BlackBerry or iPhone during social engagements was not considered rude. Amongst close friends in Egypt, smartphones were even checked mid-conversation. This new habit has proven hard to break, much to my wife's chagrin.

We checked our phones and quickly surmised something was amiss. Several of the players had received multiple missed calls from their wives, and John announced he had received three from Nora.

Receiving more than one unanswered call from the same individual was uncommon in Egypt. Etiquette required that a missed call be returned, and never once did I leave or receive voicemail in Egypt. Since only the caller pays for airtime, no one seemed willing to spend money to check their voicemail, and so it was never used. Instead, text messages arrived from polo wives: They asked their husbands to come home quickly—the protest was escalating, and the police were blocking roads. John and I were neighbors, so we left together hastily.

Our return trip to Zamalek took one and a half hours, twice as long as usual. The Qasr El Nil Bridge we needed to take spanned the Nile. Its west end terminated in Giza, the town nearest the polo field, while its eastern terminus abutted Tahrir Square. Gezira Island stood midway underneath the bridge, accessible from a single exit ramp. That day, the bridge was blocked by black-clad policemen in riot gear. They stood shoulder to shoulder, perhaps forty people wide, and prevented cars and pedestrians from accessing Tahrir and our neighborhood of Zamalek. Three rows deep, the armed policemen were intimidating. Behind them were paddy wagons. That was where we became stuck in traffic. The road rose slightly before us, and we could see that for quite a distance, nothing was moving. No one was honking their horns, uncharacteristic for Egypt. Such only happened when a road was closed, blocked to all traffic. Then our cell phones stopped working, our signal indicators both displaying an X: no service.

On the way back, we were ahead of several other players also headed in the same direction. They had been calling to ask our assessment of which route to take. We in turn had been calling Nora and watching Twitter to glean information about which roads were open. Now it was radio silence. The signal indicators on our phones went off intermittently. When we dialed anyone, we only received silence, no dial tones. I figured the cell phone system had been overloaded, but the truth was that Egyptian authorities had been attempting to turn off phone service.

Cellular phones worked intermittently throughout the remainder of the day. By the next morning, services were restored and the atmosphere on the street was outwardly normal. Two days later, by chance, I encountered Tito. He was limping and he explained that he had been shot while taking part in the January 25 protests. At the hospital, some of the pellets had been removed, but others remained embedded in his leg. The doctor hadn't had time to remove them all, as police had rushed the hospital seeking to arrest injured dissidents. Tito had slipped out the back door, and he had a video he wanted to upload to YouTube showing the evidence of the pellets in his legs. Not many knew that the police had so brutally cracked down on protests that January 25. Tito's experience was the first instance I and any of my friends knew of in which live ammunition, plastic birdshot pellets, had been used.

The series of surreal events did not end with polo amidst an uprising, interrupted cellphone service, or a bohemian real estate broker on the front lines of dissidence. Even my local convenience store made shelf space amongst the imported junk food for baseball bats, which they displayed in front of the coffee creamer. By that time, I had already purchased four bats, not for sport but for personal protection. That was the way everyone was thinking of using them, and I knew this because I had never seen a baseball field in Egypt.

16 THE REVOLUTION WILL NOT BE TELEVISED OR TWEETED

Word spread on January 26 that protestors would converge on Tahrir Square on Friday, January 28, following midday prayers. Given the violent dispersal of the rally a day earlier, I thought the confrontation between civilians and the police state would escalate. I expected stores could be closed for several days if violence worsened, so I made preparations by stockpiling food and water, purchasing a dozen frozen lasagnas from Mason Thomas, a restaurant described in guide books as a reliable food refuge for Westerners. One of its owners was purportedly Omar Sharif, Jr. Though he was the grandson of the renowned actor, he had taken the suffix "junior" as his father had not shared the same first name. He also owned Trattoria, where I and other economists assembled for our monthly roundtable.

Months later, amidst the hangover from the uprising, Sharif announced that he was homosexual and of partial Jewish lineage. One friend expected that he might not show his face again in Egypt, as homosexuality was taboo and mostly hidden from sight, especially after a gay night club was raided in 2001 and customers subjected to humiliating arrests and accusations.

That Sharif was of Jewish lineage was probably perceived as less fortunate by Egyptians than his sexual orientation. The relationship between Egyptians and Jews is storied but not complicated. The Egyptians I met universally loathed the state of Israel because of its hostile position towards Palestinians and the wars fought between Egypt and Israel over the Sinai Peninsula. As well, the Nasser revolution had made Egypt so inhospitable for Jews that today only a few dozen remain in Egypt. The worst smear to which a business could be subjected was an accusation that it was being backed by Israelis. Such libel would periodically find its way into the press, likely as a story planted by a disgruntled competitor. Such accusations had a short half-life, though, so Mason Thomas and Trattoria carried on, seemingly unaffected by the news of their owner's heritage.

In the following days, I re-watched an amateur video of police dispersing the January 25 protest.[7] I had viewed it live after being alerted of the webcast by a tweet. From the camera's bird's-eye view, one could make out erratic movements of police vehicles, protesters scattering and reassembling, and tear gas periodically wafting down a cavernous street lined by tall buildings. I presumed the repeated sounds of explosions to be the launching of tear gas canisters, but Tito explained those sounds were also shotguns loaded with crowd-control ammunitions.

I had loathed Twitter prior to January 25 for no other reason than that I had read an editorial describing it as an abbreviated form of social media for egocentrics, used to bombard others with the meaningless details of one's life. However, on January 25, Twitter was invaluable. It was an instantaneous newsfeed from citizen journalists in Tahrir Square, and protestors used the hashtag #Jan25 to relay reports of injuries, police tactics, and chants. Twitter was also a message center for protestors as they endeavored to organize. This may have been why the internet was turned off at almost precisely midnight the morning of January 28.

Or maybe the internet was turned off because of one particular email, which I did not learn of until five weeks later. Maybe the Egyptian government had intercepted it. The email contained a lengthy PDF describing in exceptional detail the tactics to be used by

---

[7] This video can be found at http://www.justin.tv/cairowitness/b/278266255?.

protestors in the January 28 rally. Its contents were surprisingly thorough and helped me understand what had happened during the days that led to President Mubarak's demise. First, though, I had to brace for what I felt coming. This I described in three emails:

January 26, 2011

Dear Investor:

Rent control, economic liberalization, and political risk are the three components of our investment strategy.

Yesterday in Egypt, protestors assembled to call for the sacking of the Minister of the Interior, who is responsible for civil rights abuses by the police, and to express displeasure with Hosni Mubarak's long tenure. The lasting impact of these protests and wherewithal of the protestors is uncertain at the moment. Protestors have been dispersed from their main assembly point in Cairo. Still, we could be on the precipice of an event that accelerates civil and political freedoms so as to join recent economic liberalizations, or we could be looking at strengthened authoritarian rule.

We highlight this quote from the following WSJ article: "For all the inspiration protestors drew from Tunisia, the demonstrations underscored important differences between the two countries. Unlike in Tunisia, where the military paved the way for Mr. Ben Ali's ouster by holding fire on demonstrators, Egypt's military has an economic interest in keeping the current regime in power. Mr. Mubarak is a former Air Force general, and the government has given top officers control over some of Egypt's largest state-owned businesses."

I am assessing the situation from Cairo and am in constant contact with Howie. We've not yet deployed capital to building purchases and will refrain until we feel comfortable that the political risk environment is satisfactory, given the return opportunity we continue to see from rent control and macroeconomic liberalization. As more information becomes available, we will share our analysis with you.

Regards from Cairo,

Marshall

␣

January 27, 2011

(Sent six hours before the Egyptian government disconnected the internet.)

Dear Investor:

The situation remains very fluid. I conducted business meetings Wednesday in the area of Tuesday evening's protests and inspected the immediate area of the demonstrations. No windows were broken or stores looted. The protest appears to have been of nonviolent, noncriminal intent. Business on Wednesday was back to normal, as if nothing had happened, though the streets were filled with riot police and paddy wagons. Yet Wednesday afternoon and evening were characterized by small, decentralized protests across the country. Thursday has so far been quiet.

However, the weekend starts tomorrow, and Friday is the Muslims' day of worship. I have learned from locals that a very large protest is to be expected later tomorrow following prayers. I believe this protest will be larger than that conducted on Tuesday.

It is reported that several hundred have been arrested. Most people seem to know someone who has been locked up for having been in the area or participating in the demonstrations, which suggests a much larger number of detentions. I remain safe, have made contingency plans, and am a reasonable distance from expected activity.

However, on Tuesday evening, the internet and cell phones were shut down for some time. I may be out of reach for brief periods in the next few days.

I had a couple of meetings today on prospective properties. It's certainly the case that there should be downward pressure on asset prices during this period of uncertainty, the duration of which remains unknown.

During this period, I am continuing to conduct business to further our pipeline by working to reach price agreements and starting due diligence. In the last few days, I've been presented an additional seven buildings for sale. We remain the only active buyer in the market. With a positive resolution to the demonstrations, I aim to put us in the enviable position of being able to move quickly to make very attractive acquisitions following the unfolding political developments.

Best regards from Cairo,

Marshall

ⒸⒼ

January 28, 2011

(Sent to my American partner thirty minutes before the internet was disconnected.)

Somewhere I lost the citation where Gamal Mubarak is supposed to give a speech. Maybe I said that? It was an internet rumor, and it turns out the facilitation that the internet leads to organizing is also allowing people to say a lot of unsubstantiated stuff. Like someone claiming water will be turned off. WTF would gov't turn off water?

Was out for a couple drinks and picked up vibe. I like action, I was a firefighter. This sounds serious though.

For quite certain, internet and communications will probably be turned off for a lengthy period tomorrow.

Know that I'm reasonably aware and I'll be safe even if you see lots of bad coverage.

Already text messaging services have been turned off and internet is intermittent.

At this point, internet and cellphones were completely disconnected. They remained inoperable from January 28 to February 2, and the only access I had to the outside world was an international phone line operated by the state-owned telephone company. It was a phone I rarely used but was fortunate to have had installed, as Egypt is a country where cell phones outnumber traditional landlines by a ratio of ten to one. This meant that during the uprising, there were only a few people in Egypt with whom I could communicate, as most only had cell phones.

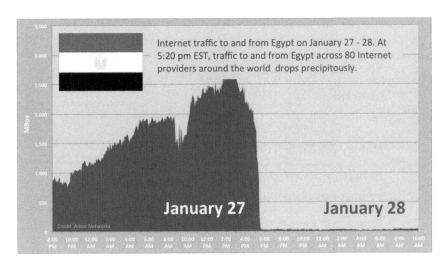

The Egyptian government disconnected the internet [8]

I kept a journal of the immediate events during the internet blackout along with my contemporaneous assessment of political interests:

[8] Craig Labovitz, "Egypt Loses the Internet," DDoS and Security Reports: The Arbor Networks Security Blog, January 28, 2011. Retrieved from http://ddos.arbornetworks.com/2011/01/egypt-loses-the-internet/.

January 28, 2011

9:05am: Basic utilities work (electricity, water). No internet or SMS service. Cell phone service looks functional, but too early to call anyone to try it out. Prayers end about 1:00pm.

9:19am: Window is open and sounds like not much activity on the street. However, the sound of a helicopter nearby is quite distinctive because I've never heard one flying about since I've been in Cairo.

9:35am: In some ways, this is a revolution against communism. The Free Officers Movement revolted in 1952 against the British, with nationalization following thereafter. One recent report said the Army controlled forty percent of the economy, making many consumer (not defense) products, such as dishwashers, bottled water, and pots and pans. Gamal Mubarak ("Jimmy," as I understand he's come to be known) threatened the Army with his economic liberalizations and reduced relative economic stature as businessmen became wealthier than the Army. The businessmen were also prominent in the Cabinet. Besides Gamal being a threat to the Army, the people are now a threat to the Army. The people are discontent with inflation, Emergency Laws, low pay, lack of political freedom, and the slow trickle-down of economic liberalization's spoils, these largely being marked symptoms of a communist economy with the latter characteristic of the oligarchy that has arisen.

So it seems to me there are three parties (economic liberalizers/oligarchs, the Army, and the people). Word is that many of the oligarchs, so to speak, have fled the country. I would too if I had their amount of money. So far, we've only seen the police in the street, being a distinctly different unit than the Army. The Army's arrival on the street would be an escalation. Thus, as I see it, we're looking at a diverse group of Egyptians revolting largely against the remaining and materially large vestiges of Egypt's communists, the Army. Mubarak the elder represents the Army.

9:56am: Last week, the currency exchange was 5.80 EGP for 1 USD. Late Thursday night it had reached EGP 5.85. Given that the EGP is unofficially pegged to the USD, I would guess that the currency reserve "basket" held by the government backing up the EGP is at least ninety percent US dollars. This change of nearly one percent in the exchange rate makes it seem like in an unpegged situation, the rate would be much more. The government must be buying EGPs now with the USDs it has in the Central Bank so as to keep the currency stable. At the bar last night, amongst the Egyptian-Americans and other Westerners with whom I spoke, there was agreed concern that there could be a dislocation in the EGP, meaning the peg could break and we would be looking at something like seven or eight EGP to the dollar. Currencies are difficult to understand and predict. Central Bank reserves and political will must be taken into account, so I'm not as concerned about the exchange rate. Those who expressed concern largely noted that their personal liquid wealth was largely in EGPs and they wanted to convert to a more stable currency (USD) during this instability.

10:11am: Looks like all cell phone service has been turned off. I have no signal.

10:12am: I have satellite with CNN, BBC, and Al Jazeera live, though the latter station is in Arabic and is replaying Tuesday's protests.

10:15am: Land line phone still works.

12:15pm: Back from having a latte—surreal, right?—and picking up an extra three prepared meals. Sounds like a call to prayer is starting. Al Jazeera live seems to have been blocked on the satellite service, though CNN and BBC World are still coming through. The latter reported that internet and cell phones have been disrupted. How about "turned off to put the country and world in a media blackout"?

12:35pm: Spoke to Ali by international landline phone to learn that Egypt's coverage is front page in the US. A friend here in Egypt reports by landline that the plan is for people to assemble at the mosques and uniformly converge on Tahrir Square.

1:02pm: A landline call from the wife of a US military officer stationed here in Egypt noted that the US Embassy has begun testing the walkie-talkie system that diplomatic staff have in their apartments but that no information has been reported via the walkie-talkies.

2:52pm: I just returned to the apartment with a shawarma sandwich for lunch. I have stockpiled food, but I figure it's best not to eat my inventory until necessary. While out, a crowd of about two hundred protesters, all well-dressed and likely upper-class residents of Zamalek, marched by while chanting slogans. The nonviolent nature of the crowd made it seem more like a parade than a protest. I assume the crowd will complete a lap or two of the island of Zamalek, imploring people to join, before heading across the bridge to Downtown, where protesters across Cairo are expected to converge. There were several uniformed police officers supervising the crowd. Disconcerting was that there were a number of *baltageyas* (plain-clothes police thugs) walking along both sides of the crowd.

CNN, BBC, and Al Jazeera continue to broadcast live, presumably unauthorized video that I am able to see by satellite TV. I also noticed that about half of the shops are open, normal for Friday, the Muslim holy day. At most shops, people are crowded around a television and watching news reports on the uprising. The ubiquity of these protests must be quite worrisome for the government. Still no sign of the Army. My friend has been trying all morning to get to Downtown to join the protest but has been repeatedly repelled by tear gas attacks as she is crossing the 6 October bridge.

4:43pm: Al Jazeera is providing live video feeds.

4:52pm: A crowd just passed my apartment and was much larger than the earlier crowd. I was able to videotape them from my balcony.

5:30pm: A 6:00pm curfew was announced on short notice. An American friend called with this news and says "Arrest or be shot" are the orders. An Egyptian friend tells me she's ignoring the curfew.

7:58pm: The Army has rolled into town to great fanfare by the protestors. The Army personnel carriers and tanks are waving Egyptian flags and giving protestors the thumbs up.

9:50pm: I went to bed early so as to be able to get out when curfew is lifted at 7:00am. I reached a friend by landline who confirmed that the Army is being welcomed by protestors. Later, though, I saw images of the protestors pelting Army vehicles. Al Jazeera is also reporting spontaneous order such that protestors are surrounding key buildings (i.e., museums, embassies, and key commercial streets) to protect them from being looted or damaged. While there were plenty of images of violence, the only looting of which I am aware is of the National Democratic Party's building, headquarters of Mubarak's political party. So far, the violence seems to be narrowly focused on President Hosni Mubarak. Foreign countries/companies are not being targeted.

[10:48pm: Email from the US Embassy in Cairo. Recipients in Cairo would not receive the email until days later, when the internet was reconnected.]

THE UNITED STATES DEPARTMENT OF STATE

January 28, 2011

The U.S. Department of State alerts U.S. citizens to ongoing political and social unrest in Egypt. Violent demonstrations on January 28 took place in several areas of Cairo and other parts of the country, disrupting road travel between city centers and airports. Disruptions in communications included the interruption of internet and mobile telephone service. The Government of Egypt has imposed a curfew from 6:00 p.m. to 7:00 a.m. in Cairo, Alexandria and Suez until further notice. Given this situation, the Department of State urges U.S. citizens to defer non-essential travel to Egypt at this time and advises U.S. citizens currently in Egypt to defer non-essential movement and to exercise caution. This Travel Alert expires on February 28, 2011.

In the event of demonstrations, U.S. citizens in Egypt should remain in their residences or hotels until the situation stabilizes. Security forces may block off the area around the U.S. Embassy during demonstrations, and U.S. citizens should not attempt to come to the U.S. Embassy or the Tahrir Square area at such times.

29 January 2011

8:30am: I am dressed and have learned from the TV that the president sacked his cabinet and is appointing a new cabinet today. This will not be sufficient. Protestors want the president gone. I would expect protests to continue.

9:00am: I stepped out and found an English newspaper and also the independent *Al Shourak* newspaper. The English newspaper contains several lengthy articles on the protests but seemingly also some material prepared before Friday's protests, like a sidebar noting the US Embassy was hosting a tennis instructor and holding a tennis camp in Cairo for the top Egyptian tennis players. Currency exchange rate remains unchanged at 5.86. There are no traffic police in sight.

At this point, I stopped my dairy and went to the apartment of my friends Nora and John. They had a view across the Nile to where the previous day's events had left burned-out and smoldering police vehicles. I returned to my apartment, where, late in the afternoon, Nora called. She suggested it was time to leave Cairo, as the personal security threat had become too great. I called my wife in America and asked her to buy me an airplane ticket. I had no way to do that over the internet, as it was still disconnected.

Late in the evening, I phoned Howie to tell him I would try to leave Cairo. My wife had called me minutes earlier and confirmed that she had been able to purchased airplane tickets for me. Both could hear gunshots in the background of our phone conversation, just outside my apartment.

I awoke the next morning to see the evidence. Spent shotgun shell casings were strewn about the street just outside my building's entrance. My bawaab explained that police forces had shot in the air to scare off thieves, and then the police had disappeared from Tahrir, my neighborhood, and the whole of Cairo. That morning, I was not surprised to learn from my wife that the US State Department had issued a sternly worded communique. American citizens had been instructed to consider leaving the country, though I would be in Cairo for two more days.

THE UNITED STATES DEPARTMENT OF STATE

January 30, 2011

The U.S. Department of State recommends that U.S. citizens avoid travel to Egypt due to ongoing political and social unrest. On January 30, the Department of State authorized the voluntary departure of dependents and non-emergency employees. Violent demonstrations have occurred in several areas of Cairo, Alexandria and other parts of the country, disrupting road travel between city centers and airports. Disruptions in communications, including internet service, may occur. The Government of Egypt has imposed a curfew from 4:00 p.m. to 8:00 a.m. in Cairo, Alexandria and Suez until further notice, and U.S. citizens should obey curfew orders and remain indoors during curfew hours. U.S. citizens currently in Egypt should consider leaving as soon as they can safely do so. Cairo airport is open and operating, but flights may be disrupted and transport to the airport may be disrupted due to the protests. Travelers should remain in contact with their airlines or tour operators concerning flight schedules, and arrange to arrive at the airport well before curfew hours.

My wife had ingeniously purchased for me three refundable airfares on three different airlines. All were still flying into Egypt during the unrest, and the tickets were for a January 31 departure from Cairo. My platinum frequent flyer status on Delta, though, was no help, as Delta was one of the first airlines to indefinitely suspend its Cairo flights and had already cancelled flights on that day.

While my wife was arranging my tickets, I had been packing as though I might not return. The situation felt dire. I learned secondhand of home invasions in Alexandria and numerous jailbreaks throughout Cairo. The police were themselves targets of protestors' angst and had disappeared from duty. My international landline remained my only two-way connection to the outside world.

Fortunately, my Cairo office had a fax machine to which my wife could deliver my tickets, though she first had to rummage through our basement to find a fax machine, as we had not used one at our house in years. I decided to leave for the airport a day early and sleep in the departures hall. Flights were being cancelled, and I figured the best place to react to flight changes was at the airport itself. I was worried that the route to the airport might become insecure the longer I waited—already a CNN report had announced that an Egyptian tour guide had been shot while escorting American tourists to the airport.

I made one last call to my wife before I went to the airport. She had found a vacancy at the airport's hotel and reserved me a room over the internet. I was skeptical, as I figured the hotel would be packed with travelers awaiting flights to leave the country, and, absent internet service, the hotel might have been unable to update its inventory. First, though, I had to get a taxi to the airport. The three taxi drivers I knew all politely declined, so I flagged a random taxi. I was prepared to pay twice or more the regular fare. Conditions were hazardous, or so I thought.

The afternoon ride to the airport was devoid of traffic. When we reached Heliopolis, where the president's office and residence were, Army tanks lined the street. The elite Presidential Guard stood along the sidewalk. Protestors, though, were kilometers away in Tahrir Square. Taxis were the only cars on the road, and the ones headed to the airport were crammed full of people and luggage. When we arrived, the meter read EGP 35 pounds ($5.83). I tried to give the driver a fare and tip of EGP 60 ($10), but he refused, informing me that he knew I would be coming back to Egypt and to keep the money for my next trip. However, I recognized that the driver was working while his family was at home during civil unrest, and I insisted he take the money. He only did when I told him I had all these Egyptian pounds and no way to spend them before I left.

I first went to the airport to see if there was an empty seat on any of the day's remaining flights. Had there been, I could have left a day early. Navigating the airport was made infinitely easier by my wife, who had convinced me to leave my two large suitcases at the apartment. I really did leave Cairo with little more than the shirt on my back.

The hotel lobby was packed. I could barely make my way to the reception desk, but when I did, they had both my reservation and a free room. They either had a satellite internet connection or had been supplied by the lone internet service provider still operating. Rumors were that the ISP supplying international markets with data from the Cairo stock exchange was being allowed to operate. Yet, the stock market was closed. I, though, still had no access to internet and cellular service. Instead, I sought comfort in food: a cheeseburger, fries, and a beer.

The next morning, I walked to the airport at eight in the morning, as soon as curfew ended. The airport terminal was a half-mile away, and police still guarded roadways approaching the airport. Breaking curfew sounded to me like a bad idea. Already, the airport was full of passengers who awaited flights and tickets. Many had gone to the airport without tickets and expected to be able to buy one on the spot. Though I was told flights were sold out for several days, throngs of people continued to arrive throughout the morning, all presumably without tickets. Finally, the departure hall was completely shut. No one was allowed in, with or without a ticket. The building was certainly beyond its capacity.

My flight departed after several hours. The curfew had caused problems for the airlines, as employees had to be given time to come and go from work. When we finally left, I overheard our British Airways stewardess explaining that they had made several circles over Cairo before deciding to land, and they had nearly rerouted the flight to Greece. As I looked out the window and saw revolutionary Cairo from several thousand feet, I consider that I might not return to Cairo, ever, as the investment opportunity may have ended due to the uncertainties of a post-uprising Egypt. I felt lucky to have left no material possessions behind in Cairo: no car, no house, and, to my great relief, no investment properties. I imagined others' anguish which came from leaving behind the material components of their life's work. Such tragedy befell Americans affected by natural disasters, but rarely, if ever, did Americans face a threat to their life's work by a quasi-anarchic political environment.

The hours I spent at the airport had allowed me to reflect on the events of the past week. I would learn quite a bit more of my friends' experiences once I returned, three weeks later, but I offered my initial impressions in a letter I penned from the Cairo airport and emailed when I arrived in America:

February 1, 2011

Dear Friends:

Being eyewitness to pervasive protests and civil unrest that are now likely to topple a long-tenured autocratic government has been awesome . . . and harrowing, but only now can I properly appreciate the passion of our American revolutionaries. It's a passion for freedom to which I wish all Americans could bear witness.

The solidarity amongst Egyptians cannot be likened to anything I've ever seen before. The protestors in my posh urban borough called themselves the "Gucci" protestors, and they looked it. Elsewhere, Coptic Christians joined Muslims, women stood beside men, and the old soon joined the overwhelmingly young group of dissidents. This was solidarity. Dispassion was absent from all minds.

Egyptians find the government's stranglehold over civil and political freedoms insufferable. The seriousness of this intolerance is greatly magnified because the Egyptian government is not the adjudicator of the dispute but the defendant, a defendant who's heavily armed. With no interest in compromise, the protestors will only stop upon complete abdication by President Mubarak and cadre, which they believe will lead to their freedom: freedom of expression, freedom of association, freedom from corruption. Lest you think otherwise, know that there's no anointed leader of the dissidents, only an idea for which they are fighting and dying.

There's too much to share in an email whose only purpose is to say, "I'm safe." That said, I am working on a travelogue. Still, a few details:

One of my employees, a young lawyer, was arrested and jailed for two days. My favorite (and most colorful) real estate broker was shot twice. He survived to give me the parting quote to this email. I shared my emergency medical technician knowledge with those setting out to nurse injured protesters and explained what medical supplies to purchase. I had restless nights with gunshots outside my apartment and have a friend who finally used her "safe" room for more than just storage. At his request, I gave my bawaab a long kitchen knife to protect our building against roaming thugs. Within hours of the police abdicating, spontaneous order arose as communities organized armed neighborhood watch groups, vigilantes. I witnessed six-year-olds wearing white armbands and carrying pipes to mimic their fathers, who'd organized to protect their property and their revolution. This revolution touches everyone. There's nothing romantic about it; it's dangerous, literally, and its goal is the noblest: freedom.

I do eagerly await my return to Egypt. I left with only the clothes on my back, a few favorite ties (I know, I know) and a carry-on with business documents. Judging by the mountains of luggage, most others seem to have left with their life's possessions. Most disconcerting is that I left behind friends, associates, and excellent, loyal employees.

"Invest when there's blood in the streets" is an occasional cliché of contrarian investors like me. Never did I think I would literally witness just such an opportunity. We were closing in on our first property, one on Medan Tahrir, the epicenter of protests and whose name translates as "Liberation Square." The best profit opportunity, social harmony and freedom, could likely lie in the immediate future for Egypt, but only once basic institutions such as the rule of law are restored. I called many friends and associates as I left Cairo, promising to come back as soon as the situation stabilized. My real estate broker, Tito, put it best: "When you return, you'll return to freedom."

Thank you for your concern, and please thank my wife. I know she did her best to keep you updated while singlehandedly managing my successful evacuation. She slept less than I did.

Best,

Marshall

Mamdouh and Bahaa, bawaabs of the author's building

17 WHAT JUST HAPPENED?

No sooner had I returned to Boston than I was interviewed live on Dennis Miller's syndicated radio show. I explained that I had witnessed armed vigilante groups protecting neighborhoods when the police disappeared. I told him what I had heard and smelled: gunshots and tear gas. I argued that dissidents wanted civil and political freedoms, not an autocratic regime. This assertion was not particularly brave.

Already, Freedom House had awarded Egypt its worst qualitative rating, that of "Not Free." In 2011, Egypt was amongst the twenty-four percent of countries with the least political rights and civil liberties. Worse, Freedom House noted that in Egypt, those freedoms were trending downward. In contrast, economic freedom had been improving rapidly in Egypt.

A young man named Khaled Saeed had died in the custody of Egyptian police on June 6, 2010, the day I moved to Egypt. Khaled had been arrested in an internet café, taken to a neighboring building, and beaten to death by Egyptian police officers. He had riled the officers when he posted a video of Egyptian police officers distributing the spoils of a drug bust. When images of Saeed's fatal injuries circulated on the internet, Egyptian Google employee Wael Ghonim started a Facebook page titled "We are all Khaled Saeed." Khaled symbolized the brutality, torture, and ill treatment Egyptians had faced under the thirty-year rule of emergency martial law.

Subway Sign (Mubarak Station is crossed out)

The Facebook page had been a medium to mobilize people for the January 25 Police Day protests. For this, Ghonim was arrested on January 28. Following his release after ten days of solitary confinement, he gave an impassioned, nationally televised interview, which led to one of the largest protests during the eighteen-day uprising.

Beating, confining, and killing activists was how the Mubarak regime had ensured its authority. According to an article in the *Egypt Independent*, an anonymous police officer claimed nearly a year after the uprising, "The Interior Ministry didn't work according to the law; it depended on people's fear of it." When my employee Shady Elewa went missing, I should have thought more of it. Shady had just begun working for me. A recent graduate, he had earned a law degree. His job was to find buildings for sale and conduct negotiations on my behalf, a task for which he would prove to be quite capable.

When work resumed the day following the January 25 Police Day protest, Shady did not show up. He did not answer his phone, either. After Shady was absent from two days of work, his step-father called me. Shady had been arrested and taken to a prison outside of town. His step-father expected Shady to be released soon and apologized for his absence. Shady later explained to me that he had been visiting his sick mother in Downtown, near the protests. He had been a bystander randomly arrested, or so he wanted me to believe. I thanked him for seeing that I had been informed of his whereabouts and condition, and I told him that Tito had been shot by police during the nonviolent Police Day protest, his legs riddled with plastic pellets.

Each of these stories was an injustice, a willful neglect of civil rights. Knowing the stories of Shady and Tito, I confidently explained to Dennis Miller that protesters were fighting for civil and political rights. Mubarak was still more than a week away from resigning, but Dennis continued and asked me to speculate on what was going to happen next in Egypt. It was as if Mubarak's resignation was a foregone conclusion.

Dennis: Give me a candid perspective. . . . It would seem to me what you're hearing from your friends that you made in Cairo is that they would hold this freedom so dear that I don't know that they would not be willing to give it up to the—you know—Muslim Brotherhood. . . . Should we worry about the Muslim Brotherhood?

Marshall: This has in no way been started by the Muslim Brotherhood. . . . There is always a potential likeness to Iran, a liberal revolution that's followed up by—

Dennis: Yeah.

Marshall: And I think everyone is sensitive to that. I don't know with any certainty what that probability is [of a theocracy]. . . . I am hoping that you get some type of rainbow coalition out of this . . . [but] you and I both know a lot of bad guys have been voted in over time.

(The Dennis Miller Radio Show, Dial Global, Inc.)

The same day I spoke with Dennis, I issued a more detailed assessment to our investors:

February 2, 2011

Dear Investor:

I have just landed in Boston. The US government is implementing a mandatory evacuation of many of its employees and facilitating the chartered evacuation of Americans. I know not a single expatriate staying behind. Since last Tuesday's brutal crackdown on nonviolent Police Day protesters in Tahrir Square and Friday's nationwide protests that defeated police forces, business has ground to a halt. Today could likely be witness to the largest demonstration yet and a nationwide general strike. The events in Egypt warrant the world's attention, as an autocratic government with a stranglehold on political and civil freedoms is about to be greatly weakened, if not deposed. This could be the felling of the Arabs' Berlin Wall.

Political risk was a component of our fund that joined macroeconomic liberalization and rent de-control. As we have reiterated in our assessment, the political risk would not come about through the electoral process but rather through a coup. I had anticipated it might be initiated by the military if a coup were to happen. The Army's goal would be to nationalize the economic value created during Egypt's six years of economic liberalization. Instead, it was the people of Egypt demanding freedom, largely political and civil freedoms as compared to economic freedoms.

Howie and I are deep-value investors. With blood literally in the streets—I've seen it—we believe there may be an unparalleled opportunity to invest at the inception of a country's systemic liberalization, a liberalization that would be far greater and broader than we expected and similarly complicated for our narrower business interest in economic freedoms. Before we can draw definitive conclusions, I need to get back in-country to assess and probability-weight the various scenarios' macro effects on economic freedom and to get back in front of building owners to collect a sense of the necessarily lessened asset prices. I hope this is within a few weeks. I want to be the first direct investor back to Egypt.

We recognize the headline risk. I have the Egyptian newspapers declaring it and some harrowing tales that will remind me for a lifetime. We've also not acquired a building, meaning "losses" currently stand at less than two percent, the amount of drawn capital. We have righted our in-country management to multiply our building pipeline manifold and possess a potentially gigantic opportunity of "time and place," given our liquidity and in-country *resources. We are about to have an additional capital closing to increase(!) our capital commitments to over $45 million after these events.*

Confounding Western media and the US government is that Egyptians are not fighting for a personality, they're fighting for an idea: freedom. We're assembling the different potential post-revolution leadership scenarios and examining their effect on political risk, economic liberalization, and rent control. We will assume risk has increased and therefore need to see that the return opportunity has similarly increased.

Warm regards from cold Boston,

Marshall

Four days after I evacuated, Egyptian Vice President Omar Suleiman was nearly killed in an assassination attempt. Earlier in the day, he had been awarded the long-vacant position by President Hosni Mubarak. One week later, Suleiman announced Hosni Mubarak's resignation and the transfer of power to Egypt's Army. The commander of the Egyptian armed forces dissolved both houses of parliament and suspended the constitution, and I booked my ticket to Cairo.

When I arrived, I immediately went to Tahrir Square. I had already spent much time there, canvasing the neighborhood for properties. I knew the square's geography well and quickly spotted evidence of the uprising. The sidewalks in Tahrir had been constructed with cement pavers set atop a sand foundation, but after the uprising, all that remained was the sand. The pavers had been removed, broken into smaller pieces and used by protestors and government forces as projectiles.

The National Democratic Party headquarters, in neighboring Tahrir Square, was also now completely burned. It had been set on fire January 29 and was still smoldering when I had evacuated Cairo days later.

The sidewalks had been broken and thrown

Very few of my expatriate friends had remained in Cairo for the duration of the uprising. My Egyptian friends were the ones whose stories amazed me. A finance executive turned dissident had been worried his employer's sympathies were with the Mubarak regime, but the stitches from a cut to his forehead had given away his participation in the Tahrir Square protests. The Globe and Mail recorded his not-uncommon story,[9] saying the protests had in part been led by middle- and upper-class Egyptians fed up with the corruption. There was other evidence that the uprising had been coordinated by those with means.

The January 27 email had been openly addressed to eighty recipients. It had been forwarded to me following Mubarak's resignation. Its author had described the attached document as "a very important piece of intel" and encouraged its widespread

---

[9] Sonia Verma, "The chameleon identity of Egypt's elite," The Globe and Mail, February 8, 2011. Retrieved from www.theglobeandmail.com.

distribution through any medium, except Facebook and Twitter. Those, he had written, were heavily monitored by Egyptian intelligence. The twenty-six-page document enumerated dissidents' demands, described how to assemble a large crowd by encouraging bystanders to join, listed strategic objectives, and pictured tactics to defeat Egyptian security forces.

"The demands of the people of Egypt" were listed as follows:

1. Overthrow of Mubarak's rule and his ministers
2. Repeal of the emergency law that suspended civil rights
3. Freedom
4. Justice
5. Formation of a new government
6. Sound management of all resources in Egypt

National Democratic Party Headquarters still burning on January 29, 2011

"Egypt Free" graffiti, post-Mubarak, February 2011

The document listed commandeering Egypt's radio and television station as the first priority. An aerial picture of the building was included and approaches marked. Dissidents were to use national broadcasts to announce the liberation of the country from the Mubarak dictatorship. That was the same tactic Nasser had used.

The second objective was to blockade the Presidential Palace. Other goals included capturing police stations and regional government offices. The plan was ambitious, but none of the strategic objectives would be accomplished.

The majority of the document described how to tactically deal with the Egyptian security forces. The necessary clothing was pictured, and substances like Coca-Cola and vinegar were recommended to minimize the effects of tear gas. Pot lids were suggested as shields from police batons, and it was recommended to spray aerosols, like spray paint, in the faces of policemen. Protestors were to approach government facilities while carrying flowers, yet there was little confusion as to whether the confrontation was meant to involve violence: Tactical goal number twelve was to seize the weapons of security forces.

Those who did not want to protest in the streets were encouraged to provide open access to the internet through their home Wi-Fi routers and to display the Egyptian flag from their home balconies.

The document helped explain what had just happened. So too did one of my employees, Tamer Hamdy.

On April 24, 2012, I was in Tahrir Square with Tamer. He was my newest hire, and, like Shady, he was tasked with locating buildings for sale and negotiating with building owners. He was a capable salesman who had already revived several negotiations in which I had reached an impasse. During my interviews with him, he exuded optimism that Egyptians had become masters of their own destiny as a result of the uprising.

We had just finished a tiring day walking around Downtown to assess several buildings that were offered for sale. I went to Tahrir that day to buy a t-shirt with the image of Hazem Abou Ismael, the radical, conservative Islamist whose mother's American citizenship had disqualified him from the presidential race. Abou Ismael had become a joke to most observers except the hardliners. A t-shirt would serve as a souvenir to my experience living amongst people whose vile hatred of America was hard to rival.

Tamer came with me to Tahrir. I sensed he wanted to ensure my safety. From a corner of Tahrir offering a good view, we stopped to take in the sight. A suited man was on a stage in the distance, yelling through overly amplified speakers, demanding the downfall of the military. Near the stage and loitering around makeshift tents were a large number of bearded Islamists, the conservative type who donned calf-length galabeyas.

أين تتجه تحديداً

١ - وسط البلد: مبني الإذاعة والتليفزيون

يجب إحاطة المبني من جميع الجهات ثم التسلل إلى الداخل ليتم السيطرة على البث المباشر وإعلان مفوض من الشعب سيطرة أهل البلد على التليفزيون المصري وتحريره من الدكتاتورية المستبدة. (رجاء النظام والتدبير)

ملابس و أدوات ضرورية

سويت شيرت أو سويتر (أبو زعبوط)، فهو يساعد على إبعاد غازات القنابل المسيلة للدموع عن وجهك.

غطاء حلة، يمكن إستخدامها كدرع ضد ضربات الأمن المركزي بالعصا أو الرصاص المطاطي.

نظارة واقية (يمكن شرائها من أي محل حدايد وبويات)

كوفية لحماية فمك ورئتيك من الغازات المسيلة للدموع

وردة، كي نعمل اللي علينا ونبدأ بتجمهر في منتهى السلمية.

دوكو رش، علشان لو حدث ضرب من قبل السلطات. نرش الدوكو على زجاج الجوز والمدرعات لحجب رؤيتهم وشل حركتهم

جوانتيات محارة، نساعد على حماية يداك من حرارة القنابل المسيلة للدموع

حذاء مريح للجري والحركة السريعة

161

I pointed to the largest building in the square and told Tamer that we had bid on it months earlier. The building was only producing EGP 1.5 million ($300 thousand) of income, but the asking price was a nonsensical EGP 50 million ($8.3 million), which equaled thirty-three times annual income and a three-percent investment yield. We were in the business for profits of twenty-five percent or more. I explained to Tamer that we always expected to dramatically increase rents after rehabilitating the property, and our expectation of increasing rents and vacating a number of the units had allowed us to bid EGP 27.6 million ($4.6 million) for the property.

As I rattled off these details to Tamer, I could see he was distracted. He looked up from the curb on which we were standing to interrupt me. With a pained smirk on his face, he explained to me that he had seen someone die during the uprising right at the point where we were standing. I immediately believed him. Tamer was not only refreshingly honest in all of the discussions we had, but I had also seen him in the midst of the uprising as captured in a photograph by the Egyptian newspaper *Youm Sabah*.

We reflected together. Tamer explained how the young man standing next to him had been felled by a single bullet. I presumed he had been shot by a sniper, as videos had circulated on the internet showing snipers on rooftops overlooking Tahrir Square.

Some of the violence during the uprising had been barbaric. The infamous "Battle of the Camel" occurred on February 2, 2011, when thugs rode camels and horses into the Tahrir Square crowd. They swung bats and maces at the protestors, and many of the thugs had fallen from their mounts and were brutally beaten by dissidents. I assume some were killed. Others who had been caught later gave confused testimony as to how they had organized the counterrevolutionary attack. One excuse was that they had become lost on their way to or from the pyramids. Laughable, I thought. This exemplified how difficult it would be to understand who in the government had ordered vicious attacks on protestors.

Historians will distill the causes of the Egyptian uprising, so we decided to forecast the future. We expected the post-uprising environment to have three phases: security, politics, and investment. All three would return, but when? They would certainly happen in that order. We immediately started watching what the guys with guns, the Army's generals, would do.

The author and Tamer Hamdy

The Supreme Council of the Armed Forces (SCAF) ruled Egypt following Mubarak's resignation. A referendum authored by the SCAF and overwhelmingly approved by Egyptians put the country on the path to elections. First were parliamentary elections to fill the houses of Egypt's bicameral government, and then Mohamed Morsi won a narrow presidential election.

The vote was widely believed to have been fairly conducted. Morsi captured 51.8 percent of the vote in the two-candidate runoff. A close ally of Hosni Mubarak, Ahmed Shafik, lost. A large number of votes were cast for Morsi by those who wanted to vanquish all remnants of the Mubarak regime, and there was even an Arabic word, *felool* ("remnants"), to describe those candidates. In my opinion, President Morsi began his rule with a false mandate, as he won merely because Egyptians wanted the *felool* candidate to lose. I felt that Morsi did not genuinely represent the majority of Egyptians, and for this reason, I have stopped referring to the events that began on January 25 as a revolution. Egypt remains under the authority of a minority, the Islamist Muslim Brotherhood and their sympathizers. What had just happened was an uprising. It was no revolution.

18 MISINFORMATION AND DISINFORMATION

A year after the uprising and little more than two months after being elected, an Islamist member of Egypt's parliament declared he had been beaten on the head and robbed. Media outlets covered the story, and people concluded that the security situation had worsened in post-uprising Egypt. Then the truth came out: The parliamentarian was recovering from cosmetic surgery, a nose job. His deliberately false story had been designed to explain his heavily bruised and bandaged face. This disinformation would cost him his political position, as his religiously conservative party forced his resignation. For them, cosmetic surgery was sacrilege. God's creations were not meant to be altered, even aesthetically challenged noses. Yet not every falsehood was purposeful disinformation. In the days following the uprising, many unintentionally false statements were made by the misinformed.

Ask directions of any bystander in Cairo and you will certainly receive a detailed answer. The route will always include several turns, perhaps to accommodate Cairo's many one-way streets. Not once was I answered with a shoulder shrug or an "I'm not from here." In Cairo, everyone knew how to get to where I wanted to go. Well, everyone except taxi drivers.

Taxi drivers became lost with great regularity. When they did, they were quick to ask for directions at every intersection. Taxi drivers knew what I initially did not: What Egyptians greatly lacked in sense of direction, they made up for in pride. Egyptians just had to give you directions rather than muttering a demoralizing "I don't know." So taxi drivers took directions by popular survey, asking a different bystander every fifty meters. Successive bystanders sometimes gave conflicting directions, but what mattered was the first milestone in the route. By constantly stopping at each milestone to ask again for directions, one inevitably reached his or her destination.

Using a map was completely out of the question in Egypt. Show a map to an Egyptian and you would think he was studying modern art, rotating the map several turns to decide which orientation was the most aesthetically pleasing. Reading a map was a life skill omitted from the Egyptian curriculum, just as punctuality must have been. I did not firmly determine what else had been omitted, since I never learned much more than a few facts about the Egyptian education system. For one, it was nearly the worst education system in the world: In 2012, the World Economic Forum ranked Egypt's overall education system as 139th out of 144 countries. Simply, public schools were no place for children who needed an education. My expatriate friends sent their children to the Cairo American College, a private day school, at the cost of $20 thousand per year. The compensation terms of most expatriates in developing countries covered private school tuition. Childless, I only ever peered inside one school, one that I could spy from the elevated 6 October highway. That school was a government-run primary school, like those that ninety-two percent of all Egyptian children attended.

The route from Cairo's airport into the city center was twelve miles in length, much of which was along a raised road that allowed a view into second and third stories of buildings that were just a couple of meters away. To combat voyeurs, large plastic baffles had been installed on the guardrails along much of the route. I suspected the baffles were also intended to hide the abject poverty of the Ramlet Boulaq slums. A view of people living amongst collapsed buildings in crudely constructed dwellings devoid of glass windows and plumbing was not how the government wanted to introduce Egypt to tourists. Rather, prior to January 2011, tourists were introduced to looming images of President Hosni Mubarak. I specifically remember one of him in a business suit and dark sunglasses surrounded by military leaders. What was it about autocrats and sunglasses? I had seen an identical image in Yemen, too.

At the school I spied from the elevated road each time I returned from the airport, the windows were mostly broken. There was an aged chalkboard, benches, and sometimes desks. The latter two resembled long, narrow plank boards, barely wider than the height of a book. Only twice did I pass by when class was in session. With even the brief glimpse that the drive-by view allowed, I could see that few of the all-male students were paying attention to the headscarf-covered teacher. Another group was wrestling in the back of the classroom. None had books in front of them or were taking notes.

Just as I became accustomed to receiving erroneous driving directions, so too did I come to expect Egyptians to arrive late to any scheduled event. The West's idea of being thirty minutes "fashionably late" was hardly haute couture—tardiness was simply de rigueur in Egypt. There were strategies to deal with the certainty that guests would arrive late. Hosts would announce a dinner as being "eight o'clock for nine o'clock," meaning food would be served regardless at nine. Inevitably, people would arrive about nine o'clock or much later. If it was a business meeting I was hosting, I learned to keep busy with work and not fret over the timeliness of my guest's arrival. A similar courtesy was afforded to me when Cairo's notorious traffic sometimes delayed me thirty minutes to an hour for an appointment. Being late was part of being in Egypt. For some Egyptians, tardiness was part of being outside Egypt, too.

Egyptian Olympic wrestlers were so late to their matches at the London 2012 Olympics that officials declared the matches a forfeit.

The result could not have been sadder. The athletes had dedicated their lives to training for a few moments' performance. That this fate should specifically befall Egyptian athletes was apropos.

However, I was also guilty of being willfully late. My Arabic tutor had invited me to her wedding ceremony, and the invitation was printed for eight in the evening. She explained to me that I should arrive at eight thirty, as the original time was intended for Egyptians that she expected would be tardy. I arrived at nine twenty, figuring I would still arrive in time to witness her walking down the aisle. However, I missed seeing her ascension to the altar by mere seconds. She had, in fact, been eighty minutes late to her own wedding.

Even in Egypt, there was a limit to how much tardiness I was willing to accommodate. That limit was measured by a multiplier of two to two and a half. If someone said he was fifteen minutes away, one could safely assume that, in reality, he was thirty to forty minutes away from arriving. "Five minutes" meant ten to twelve minutes. But when "I'll be there in fifteen minutes" became two hours, I jetted. Such was the case when I had invited a real estate broker to dinner. He had repeatedly suggested that I invite him for American pizza, as he had lived in America for a few years and was quick to tell me that he greatly preferred Papa John's to Pizza Hut. The evening that he was to be my guest, he arrived two hours late. By then, I had already eaten a pizza and left. One had to draw boundaries.

Before I relocated to Egypt, I had read a candid essay about doing business in the land of the pharaohs. I do not remember the author or title, but the advice stuck with me:

> Horrible traffic limited one to traveling to no more than three meetings per day, but more likely one or two meetings is all that can be realistically accomplished.

> Expect meetings to begin with prolonged small talk over tea or coffee that is obligingly offered by the host. Only a few minutes at the end of the meeting will be reserved to discuss the business issue.

Having an Egyptian "fixer" to make introductions is necessary.

Yes, traffic was horrible and small talk was lengthy, but the necessity of having a fixer was plainly wrong.

Egyptians are quite friendly and are usually willing to take cold-call appointments or make uncompensated introductions. One just needs to network and make contacts. That, of course, necessitates living in Egypt. Relying on a local partner or fixer, in my opinion, was far less ideal than being in the country to supervise and manage one's business. Principal–agent problems might not be a material issue for a jet-set journalist, but for multimillion-dollar businesses, the fixer relationship would likely be problematic. We knew firsthand of the challenges of managing the principal–agent relationship. We were not the only ones who found the need for a fixer to be a bad idea. I occasionally received word of others' unfortunate experience with local business managers, like the following:

From: [redacted]

Date: Wed, Aug 8, 2012 at 12:18 PM

Subject: Question re: US Consulate in Egypt

To: [redacted]

Hi Marshall,

I've been asked by my partner working on an embezzlement matter involving a US company's subsidiary in Egypt to inquire re: the US Consulate.

Apparently, in Egypt, to pursue a claim for recovery against a person who's embezzled funds from a corporation, the claimant must notify and seek collaboration from the Egyptian prosecutor's office. I understand that we've contacted the prosecutor but have encountered some resistance/confusion on certain aspects of our client's claim.

Long story short: We understand that the US Consulate in Egypt might be able to provide guidance or assistance with the Egyptian prosecutor's office.

Can you apprise me of a person or group at the US Consulate in Cairo whom we might contact for help? Not sure what types of service the Consulate provides, but apparently other US companies with Egyptian issues have received guidance/assistance.

Be well,

[redacted]

I offered several of my contacts at the US Embassy, knowing even the most interested effort from the consulate would not likely end in a monetary recovery for the aggrieved American plaintiff. I responded:

I hope this US law firm has already been in contact with an Egyptian litigator. The legal system here is much different and I am regularly surprised by how it works.

And probably the worst news is that enforcing monetary settlements between Americans and Egyptians adjudicated in the Egyptian court system is next to impossible. There's no bilateral enforcement treaty. Hopefully the injured party had an international arbitration clause. That's the best way to enforce a result. Otherwise there might be strategies to move the dispute into US jurisdiction for easier collection.

—Marshall

A fixer might open doors, but resolving contractual disputes with that agent can be exasperating. Contractual disputes could be expected to take five to seven years to reach final adjudication. Partly for this reason, I have recommended to foreign direct investors that they entrust their in-country operations to someone of their own nationality. This would bring both the principal and agent into the same jurisdiction, one that was certainly more efficient than Egypt's court system.

The advice that one could only expect two or three meetings per day was correct. Traffic and punctuality in Egypt were both bad enough to make this characterization of the business environment a reality. Also true was the expectation that all meetings would begin with lengthy small talk. Sometimes such conversations were remarkable, mostly for their candor. One that I remember was a formal meeting with officials at Egypt's General Authority for Investment (GAFI). I was receiving mixed messages from our bank about the application of restrictive controls on the transfer of foreign currency. I wanted to know the truth, and so too did the US Embassy, who had set up the meeting. Two of the Embassy's economic officers attended the meeting. We arrived in a heavily armored car. The GAFI's vice chairman and a regional manager responsible for interacting with US direct investors also joined us, as did a third GAFI representative who was responsible for North American investment in Mexico and Canada. I asked, as part of our small talk over instant coffee, when she had last traveled to either country.

She answered, "Never," though she hoped to do so in the future. As if to offset this unmistakable irony, she volunteered that she had traveled to Turkey more than fifty times, and her grandmother was Turkish. The US economic official with me then passed his card across the table, telling her to call him. He wanted to arrange a US taxpayer–funded trip for her to the US, presumably to help her better relate to foreign direct investors from North America. How was it that US taxes were paying for Egyptian bureaucrat travel budgets?

When I learned the US government planned to fly recently elected Muslim Brotherhood parliamentarians to the US for meetings, I knew that, too, was money out of my pocket. The saying "Keep your friends close but your enemies closer" came to mind. Funding the Brotherhood's travel was apparently the easy part. Many of the newly elected parliamentarians had been previously identified by Hosni Mubarak's organization as terrorists, and that Egyptian list of terrorists had been shared with the US government, so special State Department waivers were needed to issue travel visas to Brotherhood parliamentarians.

Small talk was fueled by one of three drinks: hot tea, Nescafé instant coffee, or Turkish coffee. I avoided the latter even though I enjoyed it socially, as I had noticed that the unfiltered nature of Turkish coffee left grounds on my lips and teeth, and I did not want that to be a distraction to those listening to me. I instead regularly drank Nescafé, black.

The only bit remarkable about Nescafé was its logo. Otherwise, it was a rather bland coffee. When I was pictured in the New York Times in front of Tahrir Square's revolutionary graffiti, a "NoSCAF" phrase was painted just above where I was standing. It looked identical to the Nescafé logo, but the graffiti called for the sacking of Egypt's military junta.

Directions were usually erroneous in part and estimated arrival times overly ambitious, but I worked around it. These were cultural norms. Just as with tardiness, I became accustomed to misinformation. Disinformation, however, was a different matter. Disinformation was deliberately false information meant to obscure the truth and was far more nefarious than misinformation.

One of the most damning instances of the Mubarak regime's contempt for its subjects occurred early in the eighteen-day uprising. The state television station broadcasted purportedly live images of Tahrir Square and the surrounding area, though those images had actually been previously recorded. Streets were shown to be empty and viewers were to believe reports of large crowds amassing in Downtown were erroneous. Al Jazeera exposed this explicit attempt to misinform the Egyptian populus. The Qatari-based television station showed the live images from Tahrir juxtaposed with the images state television claimed were live. The contrast should have been laughable—in that instance, it was Orwellian. Still, there were plenty of other examples of disinformation that offered comedic relief against government-scripted disinformation.

On weekend mornings when I was not playing polo, I started my day with an Americano at Costa Café. The drink was close to the drip coffee I favored in America and was a mixture of espresso and hot water. There, on the corner of a major intersection, the café's glass storefront offered a fishbowl view on life. My regular perch was a corner seat in Costa's three-table non-smoking section. My eight o'clock arrival time assured me of its availability and also provided the most interesting scenes, the most memorable of which was a beggar's secret.

The Nescafé logo was modified to protest the rule of the
Supreme Council of Armed Forces
(The author, Tahrir Square. Photo by David Degner)

The store's full-length windows were a target for beggars. Really, though, I only recall one woman and her technique. She was quite old, perhaps eighty years in age. Her face reflected years in the sun, and her wrinkles were deep. She looked poor and signaled it, too. She would tap on the window that separated her from the café's guests and gesture toward her mouth as if she was hungry. Some guests gave her change as they left, though I did not, as I had seen her secret early one morning, when she arrived in an air-conditioned taxi. She had money to pay for the most expensive public transportation mode in Cairo! Even my lowest-paid employee, my office butler, never took taxis, as he could not afford the luxury. As I had seen in a city where everyone sees something, this beggar was in no need of alms.

I was regularly subjected to disinformation in the normal course of business. Building sellers wanted me to believe they had multiple buyers who had offered obscenely high prices or that other buildings had recently transacted at prices well above reality. Separating truth from falsehoods was possible but took time. The techniques I found best were to 1) seek an indifferent source of the information, 2) subtly bring up the uncertain fact to see if the principal owner of the information objected to my seemingly factual statement, or 3) rely on financial models to test if quantitative data points, like prices, were sensible.

Indifferent sources of information included service providers such as lawyers and accountants. They, for example, participated intimately in property transactions and observed the real sale price of a property. With no publically accessible database of property transactions in Cairo, one needed to find a participant in the transaction. Yet information obtained directly from a seller was sometimes unreliable. I found that building sellers usually over-reported true sale prices. This was a boast much like that of the fisherman who sheepishly lies about how big a fish he has caught.

The Egyptian uprising of 2011 may have reduced the instances of disinformation issued by the government. Perhaps the most notable outcome has been an explosive growth of independent newspapers. The new newspapers have been quick to identify many instances of government-issued disinformation. However, at the same time, the newfound press freedoms came with a dose of misinformation. The new media has been prone to printing poorly sourced or libelous stories. Perhaps because of the now increasingly libelous press or an authoritarian streak in Egypt's new president, Mohamed Morsi, there has been a huge growth in the number of defamation cases in post-uprising Egypt. Six months after his presidency began, Mohamed Morsi was the beneficial plaintiff in twenty-four claims of defamation. According to the Egypt Independent, in the previous 115 years, only fifteen such cases had been filed.

In the end, I hope the media's new role in exposing disinformation serves as a lasting outcome of Egypt's uprising.

Propaganda: "The Army and the Police and the People Are One Hand," signed the People of Egypt

19 YOUR MONEY STINKS

In the aftermath of the Police Day protests, Downtown was labeled a war zone in Western media. At that time, protestors had not yet defeated Egypt's internal security forces, but they would do so on January 28. The "war" would cause all but the most basic economic activities to cease until February 11, the day President Hosni Mubarak resigned. Afterwards, business was slow to return to normal, and much of it never did during my two-year post-uprising tenure in Egypt. The economic consequences of the protests would be shocking and enduring.

I had braced for the events, as had others, but there were already difficulties. Friends reported on January 27 that a number of ATMs were out of order, presumably emptied of cash. Egypt was a largely cash-based economy, and having currency was critical. I had fortunately been in the habit of keeping several thousand dollars in an office safe for out-of-pocket expenses, but those thousands were in one-hundred-dollar American bills, no good if currency exchanges were to be shuttered for an extended period. That was one of the most important lessons I took away from having lived through a civil uprising: Keeping currency on hand is important, but small bills are just as important as any dense, portable store of value. There was a malodorous side-effect though, as the smell of all the small bills was particularly unpleasant. Fortunately, unlike a friend of mine, I did not have a large amount of currency or stench to deal with.

I had returned to Egypt little more than a week after Mubarak's resignation. The Army had taken over leadership of the country and kept in place the cabinet that Mubarak had reconstituted on January 31 in his failed attempt to placate protesters. The Cabinet consisted of thirty-five ministers, a number I thought excessive compared to the fifteen secretaries in the US Cabinet. This difference reflected Nasser's socialist government ideology, which aimed to control most aspects of life. Religion, sports, culture, and information were a few of the portfolios warranting additional ministers.

For rational reasons, few ministers in the new cabinet were making decisions in the post-uprising environment. Ministers presumably recognized their political tenure would be short, and few wanted to have their decisions judged by a successive government. Members of the previous cabinet were already being arrested, accused of corruption or wasting state assets, so Egypt's interim government played hot potato and hoped to pass accruing problems to the first post-uprising elected government. With ministers not making decisions, neither were bureaucrats or law-enforcement officials.

A most obvious consequence was a dramatic increase in illegal construction. For my friend who ran a cement company, business was booming. His business had become an entirely cash-based endeavor. Banks had been closed for nearly a month and did not reopen until more than a week after Hosni Mubarak's resignation. His safe came to be completely filled with Egyptian pounds from the copious amounts of cement his firm was selling. The smell, he said, was horrible. Since only one in ten Egyptians had a bank account, most everyone regularly kept cash on hand. Most paper currency demonstrated this, too, being folded, worn, soiled, and, most notably, smelly after having spent most of its life in a clothes pocket.

In post-uprising Egypt, there was only one perceptible economic policy: a stable exchange rate. I gathered that the average Egyptian understood exchange rates. They knew that a decrease in the value of the Egyptian pound would increase the cost of living, and this made the exchange rate an indicator of the government's competency. Yet very few understood why the exchange rate fluctuated.

Like all goods, the free-market price of a currency is determined by supply and demand. For the Egyptian pound, demand cratered as a result of the instabilities. In February of 2011, the month Hosni Mubarak resigned, the Central Bank of Egypt (CBE) reported its largest monthly decline in foreign currency reserves since 2005. The demand for Egyptian currency normally came from tourists and foreign investors, but both had disappeared. Hotel occupancy rates declined to four percent, and direct investors were not only canceling new investments in the absence of a civil government but were also attempting to remove money from Egypt. Likewise, foreign investors in the stock and bond markets were net sellers of their holdings. This necessitated that proceeds from asset sales denominated in Egyptian pounds be converted into foreign currency before repatriation.

To keep the price of the Egyptian pound from plummeting further, the CBE purchased billions of Egyptian pounds using the foreign currency it held. The CBE was buying enough of the Egyptian currency, but should its foreign currency reserves have proven insufficient to meet a sustained purge of the Egyptian currency, the exchange value of the Egyptian pound would drop. Already the CBE's foreign currency reserves had dropped sixty percent, and the selling pressure on the Egyptian pound had not abated. Still, the exchange rate held steady, but not without the help of other blunt tools that began to affect the livelihoods of all Egyptians.

There is a prescription for defending a currency: 1) Use government foreign currency reserves to buy the excess local currency being sold, 2) sell local currency (Egyptian pound) government bonds paying very high interest, and 3) balance the fiscal budget to prevent spending deficits from devaluing the local currency. There was a fourth tool, but it was crude: Prohibit people from removing foreign currency held within the country.

Interest rates on Egyptian government bonds increased from nine to fifteen percent, but this was not enough. Statistics indicated that in post-uprising Egypt, few foreigners were buying the Egyptian pound—denominated debt. Had foreigners bought the new debt, they would have increased the demand for Egyptian pounds, lessening the pressure on the currency. Instead, Egyptian banks began buying the debt using Egyptian pounds they held as cash deposits. When the banks ran out of excess cash for such purchases, the government reduced the minimum amount of cash banks were required to hold for potential withdrawals. It was a risky move. Those assets were increasingly Egyptian government bonds, and a fiscal misstep by the Egyptian government could mean an unwillingness or inability to pay its debts, which would lead to a run on the banks.

The Egyptian government needed to borrow money, as it was spending more than it was earning. The subsidization of commodities consumed an increasingly large percentage of the budget. That had been the situation for more than a decade. Cooking oil, wheat, and refined fossil fuels represented the bulk of the government's subsidy policy. Egypt produced some quantity of these goods, but nowhere near enough to meet local consumption. Therefore, the Egyptian government imported large amounts of these commodities.

Foreign wheat sellers sold their product in rubles or dollars, as they would not need Egyptian pounds in their home countries. The same was true of the refined diesel and gasoline Egypt imported. For this reason, the Egyptian government needed to secure a sufficient amount of foreign currency every month to pay for the imported goods it subsidized. When the government attempted to reduce the withdrawal of foreign currency from the country, it became its own worst offender.

The prohibition on removing foreign currency from Egypt was thinly veiled as an attempt to limit corrupt members of the former regime from transferring their wealth to more hospitable jurisdictions. When banks re-opened after the uprising, foreign currency withdrawals were limited to $10 thousand. Furthermore, cumulative withdrawals from the account could not exceed $100 thousand. Those rules were purportedly for Egyptians only—foreigners faced other obstacles.

My concerns were magnified when I learned the CBE's deputy governor had repeatedly said, "I can block the small number of requests to wire a million dollars out of Egypt. What I'm worried about is the large number of requests for small amounts of foreign currency." The unpublished capital controls on Egyptians made perfect sense given the CBE governor's singular goal: to prevent too much foreign currency from leaving Egypt and thereby causing the collapse of the Egyptian pound. I learned in the months immediately following the uprising that Egyptians were having trouble wiring money abroad. One of my lawyers had purchased an apartment in Geneva, but, following the uprising, his bank refused to accept documentary evidence supporting the wire transfers he needed to pay his mortgage. Others were unable to wire funds abroad to pay for their children's foreign tuition bills. Soon, I began to hear about "the ask," but not before a government directive increased the difficulties of securing foreign currency to Egyptian business.

An average of $5 billion in goods was being imported to Egypt per month, though not all was imported by the government. This meant that businesses importing goods to be sold in Egypt devised a surreptitious way to move foreign currency out of the country: inflated import invoices. For example, an executive of an import company could move money out of Egypt by paying for far more imported product than was actually delivered.

Months after the uprising, the CBE issued a directive that all bank wires to fund imported goods required sufficiently accurate invoices. In reality, the directive proved carte blanche to delay or prohibit foreign currency transfers. Frustrating delays of legitimate business transfers became de rigueur.

We had brought about $800 thousand into Egypt in August 2011 to fund the acquisition of our first building. Prior to this, we had never had more than $30 thousand in cash in the country. We were a private equity fund with a "hurdle," a minimum rate of profit we needed to achieve prior to collecting our share as managers. The profit hurdle was only to be calculated while we were in possession of investors' money. Therefore, holding cash was not ideal, though nor was relying on Egypt's banking system. We only learned this when the seller of our first acquisition made an eleventh-hour change and demanded offshore payment.

Egyptians were finding it exceptionally difficult to move money offshore. The seller was Coptic Christian, his adult sons pushing for the sale of the building. They wanted to move their family wealth out of Egypt, even though they made protestations to the opposite. They were committed to residing in Egypt; Copts were the oldest Egyptians, they said. Their names reflected this belief, as the father and two sons were named after ancient Egyptian pharaohs, a tradition of the Copts that reminded the ninety-percent Muslim majority that the Copts had called Egypt home first.

Save for the bit we had transferred to Egypt for our first acquisition, all of our capital was outside the country, literally in our investors' bank accounts, waiting for us to purchase buildings. For each building, we budgeted an amount twice the purchase price for paying tenants to vacate and restoring the building. We expected to transfer dollars to Egypt and convert them to Egyptian pounds to pay those expenses, and that was precisely the type of foreign direct investment transaction that would have bolstered the CBE's foreign currency reserves and relieved pressure on the Egyptian pound. We easily could have repurposed the $750 thousand that we had in Egypt for the building's redevelopment expenses and used a portion of the outside money to fulfill the seller's new purchase term: offshore payment. That we could easily pay for property offshore would become a major point of other ongoing negotiations.

We were assured by Egyptian government officials that no banking restrictions existed on foreigners or on Egyptian companies wholly owned by foreigners, but I had heard otherwise. An American who managed a large multinational had retired or been transferred after a long residency in Egypt, and he had accumulated $9 million of compensation in an Egyptian bank account. Unable to successfully transfer the funds abroad, he needed the intervention of his country's ambassador. An Anglican clergy member had also had trouble transferring a much smaller amount to fund a real estate purchase in England. I sensed the situation was worsening. We decided to prove that we could wire money abroad without restriction before moving forward with our investment plans.

Soon I needed to complain to the CEO of one of Egypt's largest privately owned banks. His institution had been party to my troubles in moving the $750 thousand out of Egypt. He suggested I open multiple accounts, seven more, to circumvent the $100 thousand per account limit. That might have worked in this single instance, but our project was to be nearly $50 million in size. Five hundred individual accounts would have been a red flag to regulators, not to mention commercially unfeasible. Instead, there was a more popular solution of which I learned: the shell company transfer.

Shortly after the uprising, Egyptian companies were formed to hold one asset, a sizable bank account. The company would then be sold at a discount to the cash value, purchase price paid offshore. The discount was purportedly fifteen to twenty percent. The buyers, I was told, were Gulf Arabs. Buyers of these shell companies must have had reason to believe they could not only exceed the $100-thousand withdrawal limit but also repatriate the funds to their Gulf states. That may have explained why I had heard rumors that diplomats were ferrying money out of Egypt—as a diplomatic courtesy, their bags were not inspected.

I simultaneously began hearing of other novel ways large sums of foreign currency were being moved out of Egypt. "Sealed diamonds" came in a small container, purportedly with an authoritative seal validating the number of carats carried inside. A Palestinian jeweler I had bumped into acknowledged the increased demand for diamonds, as they were an exceptionally dense store of value, one easily transported.

I also learned that the Swiss franc came in a thousand-franc bill. One million dollars could be transported in a stack of francs about four inches thick, while the same in hundred-dollar bills would have been ten times thicker. Very expensive watches and gold bullion were also used, I am sure, as a horologist I met by chance confirmed that his business was doing quite well post-uprising.

A most desperate attempt to move money was "the ask." An American Embassy official repeated to me a conversation that exemplified this tactic:

Egyptian businessman: Hey, Greg. You know my business. I import commercial goods for a living, American goods. I have a shipment coming, but my Egyptian bank refuses to wire the money out.

American Embassy official: So what's the problem?

Egyptian businessman: I don't know why the bank is refusing to wire the money. Seems like everyone is having this problem. Since these are American products, I thought maybe you could help.

The Egyptian businessman pulled out a two-inch stack of hundred-dollar bills.

Egyptian businessman: Can you take this to my brother in America so he can pay the invoice?

Undocumented movement of money was against US law, so "the ask" was ridiculous. It was also indicative of how desperate Egyptian individuals and private businesses, in particular, were to transfer currency. Evidence was also beginning to suggest that the Egyptian government was having foreign currency–related troubles. Gasoline shortages came first. Then the lights went out. Rolling blackouts began sweeping Egypt. With no official explanation given, that which was simplest was likeliest: Most electricity in Egypt was provided by oil-fueled turbines, and the Egyptian government was finding it difficult to secure fuel to power the generators.

Egypt has crude oil, but not enough. In the sixteen-year period of

1984–1999, daily crude oil production ranged from 800 thousand to 920 thousand barrels. This was enough to satisfy local demand, which grew from 406 thousand to 563 thousand barrels per day over the same period. Excess was exported.

By January 2011, daily crude oil production had fallen to 575 thousand barrels per day, thirty-eight percent lower than the high of 1995. The daily consumption rate by the time of Egypt's uprising had nearly doubled, up eighty percent since 1995. Consumption exceeded local production by 279 thousand barrels per day, and the shortfall was an expensive problem for the Egyptian government, which was wholesaling gasoline and diesel fuel well below international prices.

In 2012, a gallon of diesel fuel sold for $0.68 in Egypt, compared to $3.97 in the US. Egypt was the thirteenth cheapest country in which to buy diesel fuel of the 168 tracked by the World Bank. Of the twelve countries with lower-priced diesel fuel, all were net exporters of crude oil. Of net importers, Egypt had the lowest-priced diesel fuel.[10] Those facts presented the Egyptian government with a very big fiscal problem. It had to buy refined fuels on the open market and resell them to the Egyptian populus at a heavily discounted price, a price amongst the lowest in the world.

Fuel subsidies in 2011/12 accounted for seventy-one percent of total subsidies in Egypt, nineteen percent of total government expenditures, and six percent of GDP. The cost of the subsidy was estimated to be EGP 95.5 billion ($15.9 billion). Not only did the government need to fund the expense, but it also needed to use more than $1 billion monthly to fund petroleum imports. Yet, in post uprising Egypt, dollars were increasingly hard to find. The plummeting of tourism and foreign investment meant the Suez Canal revenues were perhaps one of the best sources of foreign currency, but those were only about $5.3 billion annually, hardly enough. Egypt was running out of foreign currency to buy subsidized goods,

---

[10] Technically, Bahrain had the lowest-priced diesel fuel of all net crude oil importers. However, Bahrain was barely a net importer, with daily consumption exceeding production by a mere 3 thousand barrels.

particularly fuel.

Save for a few months during which the Egyptian government secured foreign currency loans from external lenders, foreign currency reserves steadily declined for nearly two years after the uprising. Those loans had only bought time: The subsidization of fuel, edible oil, and wheat was a social contract that had to be broken. That necessary occurrence could topple Egypt's fragile new Muslim Brotherhood government, so they were trying to do anything except normalize subsidies, including begging.

20 BLOOD IN THE STREETS
AND A TEAR-GAS HANGOVER

I witnessed the brutality of a police state and martial law, and I hope never to see it again.

Our Egyptian property associate, Shady Elewa, had identified a building for sale one block from Tahrir Square. With ongoing skirmishes between Egyptian soldiers and civilian protestors, we opted on December 18, 2011, to meet the seller at his suburban home.

Although in his mid-twenties, Shady had only recently begun to drive. His car was a Russian Lada station wagon, a communist-era relic, which rode and sounded like a John Deer lawn tractor. The missing windshield wiper blades were of no consequence, as the number of days it rained per year in Cairo could be counted on the fingers of one hand. However, he struggled with the car's manual steering and drove cautiously.

The best route from our office took us through a large road exchange, a spaghetti-like assembly neighboring the Egyptian Museum and Tahrir Square. The route was a bit risky, but we chanced that the periodic conflicts between protestors and soldiers would remain confined to nearby Tahrir. We were wrong.

We drove south along the Corniche, the road neighboring the Nile, and came to a stop at an intersection. A quick left turn and we would head up the ramp to the 6 of October road and away from our dangerous proximity to Tahrir Square. The structure of the intersection meant we could not see to our left, the direction of Tahrir, as a low wall blocked our view. We waited for an opening before turning left, but there was no policeman to direct traffic, and oncoming cars had the right of way. As we idled, men and women began rushing by us, running from the direction of Tahrir. Traffic moved forward, and Shady struggled with the car's tractor-like steering to turn left. When I could see toward Tahrir, I was terrified. A wall of soldiers, clad in riot gear, was charging directly at us from no more than one hundred meters away.

Windshield wipers optional

The running civilians were being chased from Tahrir, soldiers in pursuit. I heard gunshots. We were in "no man's land," the space between the pursuing soldiers and the fleeing protestors. Shady seemed to freeze when he realized that the on-ramp we wanted was behind the advancing soldiers. Perhaps he was considering completing the left turn and threading his way through the sea of soldiers to reach it. Regardless, we were staring dead straight at hundreds of soldiers running full speed towards us. I instructed Shady to keep turning and make a complete U-turn, as I figured this would allow us to head out of harm's way along a path parallel to the advancing soldiers.

As Shady reversed, I looked out my window to see that the mass of soldiers had halved the gap. The more fleet of foot had broken ranks, sprinting ahead to reach straggling protestors. Then I saw it, right in front of my eyes. No more than three meters from my car window, a solider clubbed a retreating man on the head. I could see the man was a pauper, and he had one eye bandaged in gauze. The injury was likely the result of having been struck in the eye by crowd-control projectiles, and many dissidents had lost their eyesight to such injuries. He collapsed to the ground next to the car as his hands rose to shield his head. The soldier continued to repeatedly club the now prone man. Then it was over. The protester went motionless as Shady piloted us away.

We spent the next hour and a half taking a circuitous route to our meeting. We arrived almost two hours late. The next day, I read in the local paper of a "blue bra" woman, and graffiti images of a blue bra sprang up around town. The image would become the symbol of the Army's brutality toward nonviolent protestors, and an irrefutable video was circulated on YouTube as evidence, collecting more than four million views. It showed an Egyptian couple near the Egyptian Museum. They were in direct sight of Tahrir, no more than two blocks away from the center of the demonstration. As we U-turned, we must have been two hundred meters away from what befell them.

The video began as the woman stumbled. Her male companion then attempted to drag her away from a second wave of soldiers, who were joined by black-clothed police forces. Both must have been behind the first wave of soldiers I had witnessed. The woman was clad in the conservative black abaya, which had surely slowed her pace and was perhaps the reason she stumbled to the ground. Reaching the couple, the soldiers and policemen began clubbing the man and the woman. The man fell to the ground and assumed the fetal position to protect himself as soldiers repeatedly clubbed him. The last blow was delivered by a soldier who jumped in the air and landed both his booted feet on the man's chest. The woman similarly struggled to protect herself from the five men dressed in military fatigues who swung clubs at her. One repeatedly kicked her in the head until she stopped moving, her body going rigid. I recognized the odd pose of her limbs from having watched American football players knocked out by blows to the head.

Two of the helmeted policemen attempted to drag her limp body away. Their efforts caused her black abaya to slip over her head and reveal her clothing: jeans and a blue bra. Then, the inhuman happened: A third man, clad in what appeared to be a police-issued chest protector and helmet, stomped squarely on her exposed abdomen. His jeans, white sneakers, and incomprehensible actions may have belied that he was a thug hired to supplement the police forces, but the exact circumstances of what transpired were never explained in public. No one was held accountable, especially not the military junta that was ruling the country at the time.

Several months earlier, I had been trapped by similar police action. Shady and I had gone to a building across the street from the Egyptian Museum, where we had planned to negotiate the apartment building's sale price. Before we even arrived, Shady was concerned. A friend had informed him that a conflict was brewing less than two hundred meters away, in nearby Tahrir Square. We cautiously approached the building from a side street that would allow a quick escape if the situation looked grim. When we could see nothing amiss, we ascended to the building's top floor and began the meeting. Thirty minutes later, the conflict started. Two separate groups were fighting, and the police became involved, lobbing tear gas into the scrum. It was March 9, 2011, and a picture I snapped of the melee clearly framed the tourist entrance to the Egyptian Museum. There, Tutankhamen's gold mask was on display, as were a stream of Army soldiers, some of whom would perform the nearly unspeakable that day, conducting virginity tests on female activists.

While dispersing a sit-in in Tahrir on March 9, the Army arrested a number of female activists and took them to the Egyptian Museum for interrogation. After repeated denials, a spokesman for the country's ruling committee of Army generals admitted that the women had also been subjected to virginity tests while detained. He claimed the tests had been carried out to protect the Army from eventual accusations of rape by proving that the women were not virgins in the first place. Of course, that reasoning was illogical, since it implied only virgins could be victims of rape. Nine months later, an Egyptian administrative court ruled the virginity tests had indeed happened and banned the tests. The army doctor who conducted the tests was acquitted, and not a single person was held responsible. I was disgusted and wondered what I was still doing in Egypt. Two months later I learned how little a life was worth to the Egyptian government, and I was forced to again consider whether boycotting business in Egypt was the best course of action.

In an earlier May 2011 sectarian clash, conservative Muslims known as Salafis had claimed a Christian woman was being held against her will, purportedly because she wanted to convert to Islam. Three churches were burned in the Imbaba borough of Cairo, and fifteen people were killed. The Egyptian police had failed to intervene and prevent the escalation of violence. Perhaps meant as an apology for the state's failure, the Egyptian government offered the family of each murder victim EGP 5,000 ($833), a meager sum that amounted to barely more than six weeks' income for the average Egyptian. At the time, Egypt's per-capita income was $6,600. In Bangladesh, where the per-capita income was a much lower $2,000, the government had offered $2,500 in compensation to laborers who died in a factory fire.

While negotiating a building near Tahrir, the author witnessed protesters assembling near the entrance to the Egyptian Museum on March 9, 2011

These types of payments were called "blood money," and they were the necessary recompense for accidental death and manslaughter in Egypt. A lawyer explained to me how restitution was made in the instance of killing a pedestrian with one's car. Within days of the accident, one should send an intermediary with cash to the victim's family. Apologies should be delivered along with a payment sufficient to prevent the family from filing a lawsuit. That was the extrajudicial mechanism and cultural expectation for resolving unintentional deaths.

In late September of 2011, barely more than six months after the uprising, I had been in Alexandria to compete in a national polo tournament. Traveling to Alexandria had become a risky proposition in post-uprising Egypt, as vandals were reportedly carjacking and robbing people on the desolate road between Alexandria and Cairo. The police squad's polo team opted not to travel outside of Cairo, being uncomfortable with the security threat to the horses they needed to transport for the matches. Their fear was justifiable. My auditor owned horses and explained to me that during the uprising, horses had been stolen, held ransom, and even killed. One of his own had met that gruesome fate. However, in spite of the security risk, I went to Alexandria largely because I would be traveling with my boarding school friend and teammate, Mohamed, for the event. He was an Egyptian whose judgment I greatly trusted.

We stopped for lunch along the way to Alexandria. When he parked, Mohamed handed me his semiautomatic gun and asked me to put it in the glove box. He had been carrying it under his shirt. He pointed out another gun in the car, a starter's pistol that fired blanks to presumably scare off an attacker. I did not think any more of the guns or that he had begun carrying one, as many of my friends in emerging markets carried a gun; their wealth made them obvious hostage and robbery targets.

The next morning, Mohamed's driver, a South African polo coach and I were in the car headed to the polo field. Mohamed had stayed behind to spend time with his three boys when the three of us were pulled over at a police checkpoint. There a plain-clothes police officer asked our driver in Arabic what we were carrying in the back of our large pick-up truck. When the policeman stepped away to consult with his fellow officers, I quietly asked our driver what the police officer wanted. He responded with one word: weapons. That was when I remembered there had been reports of weapons being smuggled to the Sinai from Libya. Alexandria was on that route.

Since the driver spoke no English and the police officers were making their way to the truck's covered bed to find a dozen polo saddles, bridles, and mallets, I turned to the South African and said, "They're looking for guns. So you know, there are two in the car." He was nonchalant. Days earlier, he had told me of vigilante justice in South Africa's farming regions, so he must have been used to having guns around. The driver did not know about the guns either, but I chose not to tell him for fear that he might get nervous and give the police officer reason to search the truck's cab. When the police officer returned to the driver's window, he slid his gold-rimmed sunglasses halfway down his nose and mumbled something to our driver. We were released, and I was relieved. I had evaded the intersection of post-uprising weapons trafficking, the necessary personal safety of my friend's gun, and suspicions that foreigners had caused Egypt's instabilities. What a mess that could have been.

Then came a particularly disturbing experience: I witnessed the Maspero demonstrations of October 9, 2011, from a rooftop bar, drink in hand. The tragedy has been memorialized in its own well-sourced Wikipedia entry. Twenty-eight people were killed, more than two hundred injured. That day, an assembly of Copts had set out from the heavily Coptic Cairo suburb of Shubra. Protestors were intent on showing their displeasure that a governor in Aswan, Egypt's southernmost city of size, had failed to respond to the destruction of a church by Islamists. The march ended outside Maspero, the state television broadcast building. Of all state-owned buildings, it was the most heavily guarded. Armored personnel carriers, rows of three-meter-high barbed wire fencing, and soldiers armed with machine guns had become permanent fixtures at the building since the initial days of the uprising. This was sensible, as the success of the 1952 revolution had been partly attributed to Nasser having commandeered the airwaves.

I presumed Coptic protestors were hoping to attract media coverage. Many Copts believed that religious injustices were multiplying in the post-uprising environment, and the demolition of the Aswan church was just one example. There were signs of trouble even before they reached Maspero: Gunshots were heard, and stones were thrown from bridges as the nonviolent protesters marched below. When they reached Maspero, their numbers were so large that the main thoroughfare along the Nile, which Maspero fronted, became impassable to vehicular traffic.

That evening, some friends and I were atop the Zamalek Hotel. In the many times I had visited the hotel's rooftop bar, I had never seen anyone checking in at reception. The hotel was a fleabag. The elevator was like many in Cairo, a budget model barely large enough to hold four people, and there was no door, though it did have a display that registered each floor. Other elevators, such as the one in my apartment building, had no such informational display. Instead, floor numbers were painted on the walls viewable between floors. The Zamalek Hotel had another feature not uncommon to Cairo: It was built on top of another building. Its nondescript architecture rested atop a belle époque building and had made no concession to aesthetics. The rooftop bar was similarly decorated, an open area with some plastic chairs and tables. What it did have was a delightful breeze. Cairo's evening winds were the most pleasurable in the world, and the bar had an excellent view, as well, overlooking the Nile and the Corniche that ran along the opposite side of the river. When I noticed a steady stream of ambulances traveling to Maspero and returning, Twitter confirmed the worst. The protest had turned violent.

With a glass of wine in my hand, I read the minute-by-minute accounts posted to Twitter. They were worse than one could imagine. Soldiers were recklessly driving personnel carriers and Jeeps through the Christian crowd, and fourteen people had been crushed to death, others clubbed. I wondered whether justice would prevail, but I should have known better. Sixteen months after the massacre, two Coptic Christians who had participated in the protests were sentenced by a military court to three years in jail. They had been found guilty of inciting violence, destroying military vehicles, and deliberately attacking soldiers. There were no indictments, let alone a trial, in the deaths of the twenty-eight Coptic Christian protesters.

Unlike with the Maspero calamity, other times I only heard the violence. Several months after the uprising, while Egypt's military remained in control of the country, friends and I were on the way to Café Riche, which had been the subject of an Economist article describing it as an exclusive watering hole for revolutionary intellectuals and journalists. As we neared the café, we heard some fireworks a couple blocks away. As it was a Friday evening, the most popular day for weddings in Egypt, I figured the noise was celebratory fireworks. When other friends arrived quite late, they explained the sounds had been a gun fight, a dispute between shop tenants and the aggressive street hawkers who crowded sidewalks. Vigilante justice was a fact of the post-uprising environment. In other more obvious cases of injustice, a cultural norm prevailed.

The legendary banker and politician Baron Nathan Mayer Rothschild is widely thought to have recommended to investors, "Buy when there's blood in the streets—even if the blood is your own." This adage is often used by contrarian investors who endeavor to purchase assets when a business environment is gruesome. The famed American investor Warren Buffet offered an analogous statement: "Be fearful when others are greedy, and be greedy when others are fearful." In times of fear, assets are often deeply discounted, as most market participants are scared and opt to hold cash instead of less portable assets like companies and buildings.

Egypt, though, was no metaphor. Blood really was in the street. So too were thuggish government security forces. The blue bra horror happened only a couple of blocks from where I had been. What was I doing? Was investing in Egypt moral? Was it ethical? I reasoned that I was doing the right thing.

The morality of our investment project was certain. In the good-versus-bad dilemma, our endeavor was good. It hurt no one, and all of our business transactions were to be voluntary, none coerced. Sellers of buildings and tenants were free to accept or refuse our monetary offers for their assets. The employees I hired were not conscripts, which contrasted to the Egyptian Army's use of forced labor, as 500 thousand conscripted soldiers made up well more than half of Egypt's Army.

The ethical dilemma proved a bit more challenging. Private Egyptians wanted to do business with me, while others wanted me to offer them employment. Those I hired sought on-the-job training to learn from my management education and experience. They wanted to build their skills. This fact was in sharp contrast to the signal I was potentially sending the ruling military junta: that beating and maiming protestors would have no negative economic consequences, that human rights were non-factors in investment decisions. These considerations framed the ethical dilemma:

Was it better to build a business offering salutary benefits that, in the long run, would enhance Egyptians' lives?

Or was it better to withdraw from all economic endeavors to signal objection to the government's human rights abuses?

I made the judgment call that continuing our investment project would improve the lives of the dozens of employees, service providers, building sellers, and tenants with whom I dealt, whereas I, a single foreign investor, was unlikely to effect changes in Egypt's policing policies. Effecting those changes would take an embargo or boycott, though even those had failed to change government behavior in most cases. North Korea and Cuba were two decades-long examples demonstrating that economic isolation does not work.

I hoped wiser leadership and democratic principles would prevail over Mubarak's police state and the subsequent martial law under which I was operating. My investors and I were taking the same calculated risk that Baron Rothschild and Warren Buffet had advised, and I steeled myself to continue conducting business when there was blood in the streets. However, my resolve was repeatedly tested. The blue bra atrocity and the clubbing of a protestor within meters of me were just two events amongst other gruesome realities and personal dangers I faced.

21 SHADES OF FORMER GLORY

We scheduled the outing for a weekday evening to avoid being caught in one of a series of post-uprising clashes between protestors and police forces, most of which were happening on the weekends. The evening started at eleven thirty, when we were escorted to one of the twenty or so tables at the club, all of which looked similarly bedecked in sticky plastic table cloths. Seated near the back of the room, I found that our view was not great. The several structural columns obscuring the stage front did not help, either. Still, we promptly ordered the first round of beers, one for each of us, five in all.

Like the Scheherazade, from which we had just come, this "nightclub" had a male vocalist who belted out popular Egyptian songs while another musician played an electronic keyboard. With ample application of electronic reverberation to the singer's voice, I counted at least three echoes for each spoken word and could not understand the Arabic lyrics. Later in the show, I heard the first word I could understand, *Amerikee*, meaning a person from the United States. The vocalist had approached our table, asked our nationality, and welcomed us to Egypt. He attempted to encourage the other patrons to clap for us, the only non-Arabs in the crowd. They did not, and I began to second-guess whether my friend should have announced that we were American.

I could see a couple of guests on the stage, dancing rhythmically to the music. Their hips moved mechanically, alternating between a fast and slow cadence and in sync with the fast-paced percussion line. Their arm movements flowed slowly and independently of the music so as to not distract the viewer from the shaking hips. Both dancers were older men, perhaps in their late fifties. One had his eyes tightly closed and displayed a large smile full of teeth. That he never opened his eyes made me wonder if I was watching a Christian Pentecostal pastor channel the spirit of God. Then the belly dancer appeared from behind one of the columns blocking my view. The second man paid her no heed as she shook her tightly clothed body near him. That prompted me to ask my friend if we had wandered into a gay bar.

The belly dancer wore tight sequined shorts and a tube top. Both were entirely too revealing of her middle-aged body and the cellulite it had accumulated. I spied the club's manager in the corner. He was a sixty-year-old man with a dyed comb-over, and his dapper outfit consisted of a tailored ivory sport coat and navy blue pocket square. Patrons were oblivious to his dashing attire, and so too was the band. The male singer wore dirty jeans and a flannel shirt that looked more like the dress of a day laborer. I was the only other one wearing a sport coat, a khaki Egyptian-brand jacket I regularly wore to carry my wallet and phone. I did, however, consciously leave my maroon polka-dot pocket square at home. My wife had warned me, for fear that I might be victimized, to not look too much like a foreigner whenever I went out and about.

The club manager signaled to the belly dancer, as if he were shooing a fly away, that her time was over, and she scurried off stage mid-song. A more attractive dancer emerged, and the two old men cleared from the stage. The deafening music continued, and the beer arrived . . . at room temperature. Not just five beers, but ten beers. Two for each of us.

This nightclub was notably different than the one we had just left.

The Scheherazade had, moments earlier, been my introduction to Egypt's "girlie" bars. There, the cover had been EGP 6 ($1), and the crowd was older. We and two young Egyptians had seemed out of place amongst the club's regulars, several of whom were openly rolling hash joints. When one in our group, a younger American employed at the Embassy, asked, "Why is that guy taking all the tobacco out of his cigarette?" I left the question unanswered when we could see the bar of hashish in his other hand.

I had leaned over to my friend and declared that the Scheherazade felt like Havana to me. I had never been to Cuba, I immediately confessed, and noted the club's interior sure looked like what I had seen in movies filmed in the modern-day communist country. The ten-meter ceiling and plaster walls were colorfully painted and chipped everywhere, and strands of red Christmas lights hung in a circle around the stage. Perhaps ten of the hundred strands were working. I could not imagine how glass in the fancy light fixtures suspended thirty feet overhead had broken. Next to the main stage at Scheherazade, four black and white posters of famous belly dancers had reminded patrons of days past. The local bar guide described the joint succinctly: "Those were the days."

At the Horreya ("Freedom") bar in Downtown, a dive popular with locals and expatriates, beer is EGP 9.5 ($1.58) for a bottle approximately twenty ounces in size. With two servers for the more than a hundred patrons, the tab was kept by how many opened bottles were on one's table. Ten bottles amounted to an EGP 95 ($15.83) bill. If you ran out of table space for bottles, you had to pay up for it to be cleared. At Horreya, I had been taught the necessary technique to accept a properly chilled beer.

Easily carrying a half-dozen beers, the waiter held the bottle by its neck. With the same hand, he simultaneously positioned the bottle opener over the cap. No sooner had the patron grabbed the bottle than the waiter would lever off the cap. Ideally, one would notice whether the bottle was warm before the waiter could lever off the top. Warm beer was not customary, as it was in English pubs. In

Egypt, it was a symptom of poor bartending.

When ten beers arrived in front of us at the second belly dancing nightclub, the waiter's technique was less clever. The bottles sat in front of us, momentarily unopened. Before he could open one, I had already declared the beer bottles felt warm and replacements were necessary. The waiter wandered off, leaving the beer on our table. He returned with five juice-sized glasses, each with two cubes of ice.

From Downtown's crumbling belle époque buildings to the thwarted hopes of the revolution, was this what Egypt had become? Warm beer served over ice cubes?

*A temporary wall to protect a government building from riots
had become another man's canvas*

22 CALLING IT QUITS

On August 30, 2012, we called it quits in Egypt. I was the one to recommend we not continue our investment efforts. I believed without a doubt that the decision was correct, given the worsening investment outlook. The finality was bittersweet, as Egypt had been part of my life for five years; I had lived in Cairo close to three years when I wound down our business and left on December 23, 2012.

We had not purchased any buildings. In the preceding months, I had negotiated on numerous properties and reached agreements on price for several, as property owners in every real estate market had become eager to sell. For rent-controlled properties that we found attractive and appropriately priced, we just needed to settle on payment terms, mostly the payment locale. We even expanded our geographic area to Heliopolis, which was not witnessing the near-weekly political protests and insecurities of Downtown. Yet Heliopolis' calm would be broken when President Morsi started consolidating power and dissidents attacked the presidential palace in the borough's center. Morsi's assumption of powers not afforded him by the constitution did not trouble us as much as what he did not do: He had not addressed Egypt's dire economic situation.

Simultaneous to my day-to-day management of the rent decontrol business, I had sought to collect insights on the economic and investment policies of post-uprising Egypt. To this end, I organized a monthly economists' dinner. There were four of us who regularly dined to swap notes and empty bottles of wine. Each had a unique perspective and connections. Mine were decidedly the most practical, as I was managing an Egyptian business and dealing with an increasingly dysfunctional Egyptian banking system. I was also privy to all sorts of business anecdotes from numerous local lawyers, brokers, and building owners with whom I conversed daily. The other regular participants included an economic officer at the US Embassy, a think tank executive director, and an investment strategist who worked for Egypt's premier investment bank, EFG Hermes. Our areas of expertise ranged from intergovernmental relations to capital market developments. We also periodically invited guests, such as journalists and employees of multilateral financial institutions, to join us. To conduct business in a country where policies were opaque, in conflict, or constantly changing, macro risks had to be continually monitored. Our talking shop helped.

The transitional government preceding that of the popularly elected Islamist president Mohamed Morsi had not assembled a respectable economic plan. I knew this, as I had seen the reform plan they tried to pass off to the International Monetary Fund (IMF). I had been asked for my comments on it, and I began by saying, "It looks like a third-grader wrote it."

Sure, the Egyptian government had done a poor job translating into English such a critical document, but the proposed economic reforms lacked any substance. When Egypt elected Mohamed Morsi as president, we expected him to address the economic conditions that had led to the collapse in reserves and shortages of commodities. Morsi did everything but address the economy. Worse, the few actions his cabinet had taken demonstrated a poor understanding of economics.

During a November 2012 visit by the IMF, the Egyptian government removed the subsidy on 95-octane gasoline. The decision was a sop toward the IMF's demand for substantive economic reform. Already the most expensive gasoline before the subsidy was lifted, 95 octane was almost exclusively used by wealthy consumers whose imported European cars demanded highly refined fuel. The prices of lower-grade gasoline remained unchanged, and the government forecasted a paltry EGP 55 million ($9.2 million) in subsidy savings. At the time, the overall fiscal budget deficit was EGP 200 billion ($33.3 billion). Government leaders needed to find 3,600 similarly sized opportunities to reduce subsidies if they were going to balance the budget.

The opposite happened, as subsidy costs likely increased. The headline in the Daily News Egypt days later read, "95 octane sales plummet after subsidy lifted." The article noted consumers had shifted their consumption from 95 to 92 octane, a grade of sufficient quality to fuel even the most finicky cars. 92 octane remained heavily subsidized and the substitution effect the newspaper described meant subsidy savings would be little, if any. Worse, if enough consumers shifted their consumption, the government's total subsidy bill might have grown as a result of removing the subsidy on 95 octane, hardly the outcome anyone desired. A policy decision like this one proved that the Egyptian government did not understand the gravity of the situation. All subsidies needed to be reduced. Likewise, the government seemingly did not understand a basic economic principle: Consumers will seek substitution goods if cost necessitates.

Egypt's series of interim post-uprising governments had two pressing economic problems: a fixed exchange rate and a structural budget deficit caused by some of the largest subsidies in the world. Both could be fixed. Subsidies could be more efficiently targeted and reduced, and the exchange rate could be floated, allowing the market to determine the EGP's price without the Central Bank of Egypt intervening as the buyer of last resort for the currency. The simplest solutions came at great social cost and were hardly creative. Instead, novel solutions that promised to minimize economic discomfort proved more attractive. They were also completely ineffective.

To address Egypt's dwindling foreign currency reserves, the government wanted to replenish its holdings by borrowing foreign currency. The Egyptian government solicited loans and deposits from foreign governments and multilateral institutions like the IMF. Both were sources of foreign currency that Egypt would need to repay in the future. The gamble would be that the monthly drawdown on foreign currency reserves could be reversed and reserves accumulated before the foreign borrowings and deposits came due. This was a doubling down, much like that done by a gambler who, after losing a hundred dollars, borrows a hundred more, hoping he can make back the losses in a subsequent series of winning bets. In Egypt's case, the causes of reduced foreign currency inflows were under the control of the government: Security problems were keeping tourists away, and political instability was worrying investors. The Egyptian government was in a good position to win its doubling down so long as it took action to address the causes. But the government did not do so.

Instead, the caretaker cabinet that preceded the election of Mohamed Morsi had proposed to sell land to increase foreign currency reserves. Minister of Planning Fayza Aboul Naga explained that land parcels outside of Cairo could be sold to Egyptians living abroad. She claimed $3 billion would be raised. Little, if any, land was ever sold. Two months later, this novel solution to Egypt's foreign currency problem was indefinitely postponed.

The most ludicrous plan to fix Egypt's economic woes was Account 333/333. Mohamed Morsi had opened a bank account (#333/333) and solicited financial donations "to support the Egyptian economy." A November 28, 2011, article of the Egypt Independent, entitled "Egypt's renaissance bank account raises doubts" noted that Morsi's idea "demonstrated the hollowness of a real economic recovery strategy." In essence, Morsi had resorted to begging.

President Morsi and his cabinet also attempted to implement tax increases. On a Sunday afternoon, Morsi signed a decree to increase taxes on a variety of consumer goods. The decree lasted but a few hours, as early the next morning, around two o'clock, Morsi posted to his Facebook page that he had rescinded the decree. Egypt's economy was rudderless.

Still, as I labeled it, our "business in a box" was excellent. Building sellers were rapidly lowering their asking prices, and tenants were under increased economic duress due to Egypt's economic slowdown. As a result, key money payments to tenants in return for vacating the apartment should have been lower than we had budgeted. Surplus labor from Egypt's slowed economy would have translated into lower renovation costs. All of our costs were going down, and the situation on its own looked like an excellent time to invest. The rub was that five years hence, we would need Egypt to be on a path to economic recovery from the deleterious effects of the uprising, or else we would not be able to sell the properties at prices we forecasted. Maybe we would not be able to sell our properties at all, or we might have been subject to capital controls that prevented us from removing our profits from Egypt. The whole project became contingent on the economic conditions of Egypt five years hence.

Then, President Mohamed Morsi further consolidated his power while his cabinet began to issue policies detrimental to investors. I summarized our intent to cease operations in a letter to our investors:

August 30, 2012

Dear Investor:

Today we have enough negotiated buildings to sufficiently meet eighty-five percent of our acquisition goals, including several buildings with asking prices now below our reserve price. The current environment has also benefited our operational model: Acquisition prices have declined, and we believe tenants will be more receptive of key money, both due to ongoing economic stress. We could immediately deploy capital.

However, at the same time that our operations are succeeding, macroeconomic and policy risks are quickly worsening and could last for much of our investment horizon, given recent political developments.

President Morsi's recent cabinet selection is disappointing. It is becoming evident that his economic policy will not correct structural imbalances and relies on centralized economic planning.

The central bank governor and finance minister were the principal architects of Egypt's misguided post-revolution policies to defend the currency peg and increase the top marginal tax rate (twenty percent to twenty-five percent). We were expecting they would be removed. Instead, Morsi reappointed both this month.

Morsi is also consolidating his and presumably the Muslim Brotherhood's power, seemingly at the neglect of his duties to the economy. Generals have been sacked, editors have been replaced, new state governors will be appointed, and reports are that judges will be culled. Egyptians demanded a systemic change, and Morsi is delivering on demands, except with respect to economic reform.

I believe pending economic and currency crises could lead to excessive investment risks that cannot be mitigated. Some arising risks could be catastrophic. Potential risks include further tax increases and the application of capital controls to foreign direct investors. Such would be consistent with the policies previously championed by the "hold-over" finance minister and central bank governor.

Reviewing the probability-weighted scenarios, I have come to the conclusion that economic freedom now appears most likely to decrease over our investment horizon. Likewise, certain catastrophic risks are now more likely, given hold-over economic officials. In my judgment, the best way to steward your investment is to recommend that we cease operations.

Warm regards,

Marshall

Weeks before I left Egypt and the project, Morsi started a constitutional crisis, having endowed himself with a wide range of powers not described in Egypt's constitution. This move suggested Egypt's Islamist president had little interest in building a democratic society. He simultaneously sacked high-ranking judges. Judges were a fiercely independent lot, as evidenced by the country's admirable ranking of its judiciary independence: 54th out of 144 countries, according to a report by the World Economic Forum. The judges might have worked at a dreadfully slow pace, but they were independent of political influence. At about this time, protestors returned to the streets in numbers rivaling those seen during the last days of the Mubarak regime. This time, though, there was no unanimity. In my estimate, protestors were evenly split, as had been the case during the presidential election, between those who supported a decidedly Islamist government and those who wanted a more inclusive government.

We had already decided to cease operations, but the constitutional crisis I witnessed during my final days in Egypt certainly meant an economic recovery would never occur within the time frame we needed for our project to be successful. Had we invested in Egypt, I doubt we would have been allowed to repatriate our money unless economic policy was dramatically righted. So we called it quits.

23 EMERGENCY MESSAGE FOR U.S. CITIZENS NO. 24

I just received "Emergency Message for U.S. Citizens No. 24" from the embassy. That's 24 specific security warnings this year, averaging one every ten days. You know, "groups . . . to protest a range of issues . . . clashes may occur . . . non-essential travel in Downtown should be avoided . . . blah, blah, blah." Booorrrring.

—My posting to Facebook on September 11, 2012

The US State Department periodically disseminated country-specific information to Americans who register to receive such notices. The communiques' subjects ranged from instructions on how to cast absentee votes to urgent security alerts. In the case of Egypt, security alerts highly outnumbered other matters. Security messages were even sometimes sent more than once per day. In 2012, security alerts averaged around one every ten days. They were constant reminders of the ongoing political violence in the two years following Mubarak's resignation.

On September 11, 2012, I had received the twenty-fourth communique of the year. Each of the previous messages had not been followed by any attack on the US Embassy or on groups of

Americans. I suspected that the twenty-fourth missive was nothing more than a consular's cover-his-ass email on a historically noteworthy day. Really, the only remarkable part of *Emergency Message for U.S. Citizens No. 24* was that it was less specific than most other previous warnings. Hours after I posted to Facebook, the American ambassador to Libya was dead and the American Embassy in Cairo defiled.

That same evening, I had just arrived at a "boys' night out" dinner, a monthly assemblage of married expatriates, mostly Spanish diplomats, when the news first came to me through Twitter. Tweeters reported that Egyptian protestors had scaled the walls of the US Embassy, lowered the American flag, and raised their own standard. John was seated next to me at dinner. He checked his BlackBerry and noted that he had received no such news by email from his employer, the US government.

Most everyone had a BlackBerry in Egypt. Many people had two or even three cell phones so as to separate work and leisure numbers. BlackBerry's proprietary messaging system was quite popular. Some believed it to be the most secure form of communication, unsusceptible to monitoring by the Egyptian government. Unlikely, I thought. I knew state department employees had been issued BlackBerrys, but their messaging service had been disabled by the US government. I was usually careful not to send text messages or emails in which I opined on political developments in Egypt.

That night I had sent a few BlackBerry messages to friends, asking what was going on at the US Embassy. Sitting next to her husband, John, at the boys' dinner, I read a message from Nora Soliman: "No Egyptian flag but the black Islamic flag favored by the like[s] of Al Qaeda . . ." That an al-Qaeda flag now flew above the US Embassy removed any doubts I had about our decision to withdraw from Egypt. If the Egyptian government could not defend even the American Embassy, there was no way Egypt's new leadership would have the will to protect investment properties privately owned by Americans.

The next morning's news was tragic. Tweeters began relaying traditional press reports: The American Ambassador to Libya was dead, killed by militants in Benghazi. None of my US government friends had heard the news, so we speculated that maybe Arab news agencies had confused the ambassador with a lower-ranking diplomat. After all, the US Embassy in Libya was in the city of Tripoli, not Benghazi. We thought it unlikely the ambassador would be at the US Consulate in Benghazi, a field office. The news soon proved true, with rather gruesome photos of the ambassador's body circulated by Arab media outlets. He had reportedly succumbed to smoke inhalation, and I could see from his body that this was likely true: There were the telltale signs of soot around his nose and mouth, something I recognized from having been a firefighter.

The death of the US Ambassador to Libya, Chris Stevens, hit me a bit hard, but I was unsure as to why. I did not know him, nor had I ever been to Libya. I read in the following days that he had been admired for his candor and approachability. In the end, I concluded that Ambassador Stevens had worked towards goals much bigger than himself. He worked at something he believed in. So had I.

EPILOGUE

My parents called on September 11, 2012, concerned by images that had been broadcast of protesters attacking the US Embassy in Cairo. I reminded my mother that I rarely went there, but, in any event, I promised her I would not lollygag at the embassy. That placated her. Parents, though, can always be counted on to give unsolicited advice. My mother ended the conversation with a priceless instruction: "Keep growing your beard."

My beard was the most visible evidence that I had gone "local." After I ended my work in Egypt, I found it hard to temper my interest in the continuing drama of the Egyptian uprising. I wanted to confirm if I had been correct in ending our investment efforts.

Egypt's economic climate continued to worsen following my departure. Foreign currency became even harder to access. The government restricted dollar and euro withdrawals at ATMs. Monthly withdrawals were capped at two thousand dollars per account. President Mohamed Morsi's administration continued to be unwilling or unable to implement a reform program, and the IMF's reaction was to further delay granting a multibillion-dollar loan.

Political disagreements worsened and devolved into nationwide protests. An Islamist professor at Al Azhar announced a fatwa, claiming that the murder of liberal opposition leaders was religiously justified. Vigilante groups attacked and killed dissidents, and a video captured eight riot policemen beating and dragging a naked fifty-year-old unemployed laborer across a street. The event was reminiscent of the woman in the blue bra. Two days before the disturbing video of police brutality was released, Egypt's Minister of Defense suggested the possibility that the Egyptian state might collapse. Time will tell.

An Egyptian saying tells visitors, "If you drink from the Nile, you will return."

I drank from the Nile.

ABOUT THE AUTHOR

Marshall L. Stocker is an American adventure capitalist. He has shared his research and experiences with a range of audiences, from readers of the New York Times to Iranian and Yemeni policy leaders. After managing emerging and frontier market investments from New York and Boston, he moved to Cairo, Egypt. There he led the first foreign direct investment group organized to redevelop urban real estate.

Stocker earned a bachelor's degree in engineering and a master's degree in business administration from Cornell University. After living through the Egyptian uprising, he now resides with his wife in Boston, Massachusetts.